UNIQUE Arizona

W9-CHQ-584

A Guide to the State's Quirks, Charisma, and Character

Tom Barr

John Muir Publications
Santa Fe, New Mexico

Special thanks to Leia James, Arizona Office of Tourism; Chuck Smith, Desert Botanical Garden; Tony Alba, Phoenix & Valley of the Sun Convention and Visitors Bureau; Jean McNight, Miriam Vasquez, Metropolitan Tucson Convention and Visitors Bureau; Peggy Collins, Prescott Chamber of Commerce; Douglas Chamber of Commerce; Lori Carroll, Arcosanti; Suzette Lucas, Taliesin West; Courtney Castillo, Yuma Convention and Visitor's Bureau; Sheldon Miller, Greater Globe-Miami Chamber of Commerce; Betsy Hoyt, Lake Havasu Area Visitor and Convention Bureau; Sherrie Petersen, Bureau of Land Management; Virginia Macy, Round Valley Chamber of Commerce; Cheryl Steenerson, Arizona State Parks; Julie Brooks, Wickenburg Chamber of Commerce; Sedona-Oak Creek Canyon Chamber of Commerce; Flagstaff Convention & Visitor's Bureau; Arizona Game and Fish Department; Colleen Hyde, Grand Canyon National Park; National Park Service; Petrified Forest National Park; Deborah Shelton, Arizona Historical Society; Jim Ballinger, Gretchen Herrig, Amy Carr, Phoenix Art Museum; Arizona Commission of Indian Affairs; Bisbee Chamber of Commerce; Glendale Chamber of Commerce; Scottsdale Chamber of Commerce; Tempe Convention and Visitor's Bureau.

John Muir Publications, P. O. Box 613, Santa Fe, NM 87504
© 1994 by Tom Barr
Cover © 1994 by John Muir Publications
All rights reserved. Published 1994
Printed in the United States of America

First edition. First printing September 1994

Library of Congress Cataloging-in-Publication Data
Barr, Tom.
Unique Arizona : a guide to the state's quirks, charisma, and character / Tom Barr. — 1st ed.
    p.   cm.
    Includes index.
    ISBN 1-56261-178-X : $10.95
    1. Arizona—Guidebooks. I. Title.
F809.3.B37 1994
917.9104'53—dc20   94-20034
                                                CIP

Front cover photo: Leo de Wys Inc./Steve Vidler
Front cover photo inset: Leo de Wys Inc./M. Uemura
Back cover photo: Eddie Goldbaum Rios/Metropolitan
  Tucson Convention & Visitors Bureau
Typography: Marcie Pottern
Illustrations: Bette Brodsky
Typefaces: Stone Serif, Oz Handicraft
Printer: Malloy Lithographing, Inc.

Distributed to the book trade by
W. W. Norton & Co.
New York, New York

CONTENTS

INTRODUCTION

Nothing but endless sunny days, deep canyons, high buttes, and flat desert. That's Arizona, right? Peer into awesome depths from the North and South Rim, take an exhilarating river rafting trip down the mighty Colorado River, or backpack and ride a burro through endless ravines, and you know right away you're in the Grand Canyon State.

Grand Canyon National Park

Enjoying the view from the South Rim of the Grand Canyon, circa 1914

Of course, there are many other things to discover about unique Arizona. Did you know that Arizona has more national parklands than any other state, that trees cover one-fifth of the land, and that it has more shoreline than the entire west coast of the United States? Did you know that in Arizona you can explore ancient cliff dwellings, search for legendary lost gold mines, and hike lands which were once strongholds of Cochise and Geronimo? Or that Arizona has the oldest rodeo in the nation, and festivals honoring its Hispanic and Native American heritage?

Unique Arizona presents fascinating facts, intriguing destinations, tantalizing trivia, handy charts, and quick access maps in a user-friendly format. Where else can

Metropolitan Tucson Convention & Visitors Bureau

Arizona's state flower is the blossom of the saguaro cactus

you find recipes for Rattlesnake Chili and Mesquite Cookies, the best place to see 14 species of hummingbirds, maps to Indian reservations, and tips for off-the-beaten-path recreation? However you choose to use this book, you'll soon find out what is unique about Arizona.

Desert Monarch

The saguaro cactus is often called the Monarch of the Desert. Its creamy white blossom is Arizona's state flower. Papago and Pima Indians used virtually all parts of the saguaro, and marked the start of their new year when its first blossoms appeared in late May or early June.

Although saguaros have become a symbol of the American West, they grow only in the Sonoran Desert of Arizona, northern Mexico, and south-eastern California. Expanding and contracting its ribs as it stores and uses moisture, a saguaro may live for 200 years and weigh several tons when full of water. The affable-looking succulents provide food for a variety of birds and bats, shade for jackrabbits, and nests for woodpeckers, flycatchers, and owls.

Arizona

Population:
3,665,000

Area:
113,909 sq. miles

State Capital:
Phoenix

Nickname:
The Grand Canyon State

Date of Statehood:
February 14, 1912

Highest Elevation:
Humphreys Peak
12,670 ft.

State Tree:
Paloverde

State Bird:
Cactus Wren

State Mammal:
Ring-tailed Cat

State Fossil:
Petrified Wood

State Gemstone:
Turquoise

THEN AND NOW

In the Beginning: 20,000 B.C. to A.D. 1450

Archaeologists estimate that humans have lived in the Arizona area for at least 20,000 years. Until approximately 4000 B.C. they hunted mammoths, mastodons, antelopes, and other large animals which fed on the then-lush grasslands.

Anasazi petroglyphs at Lyman Lake State Park

Arizona State Parks

At **Lehner Mammoth Kill Site**, archaeologists found spear points, charcoal from ancient fires, and bones of mammoths, tapirs, lions, and bison which archaic hunters killed over 12,000 years ago. *FYI:* 19 miles southeast of Sierra Vista; 602-366-5554.

Roaming in nomadic bands, and living in caves, these people left no architecture, and few tools. Two trails at **Little Black Mountain Petroglyphs** lead to over 30 examples of their primitive rock art. Spanning 6,000 years, the pictures are thought to relate to life, death, and communication with gods or spirits. *FYI:* Bureau of Land Management; 801-673-3545.

2300–500 B.C.

Between 2300 and 500 B.C., Arizona Indians learned to grow grains and vegetables from Mexican tribes, make pottery, and weave baskets. Such seemingly innocuous activities represented a cultural revolution and brought wholesale changes in their lifestyles. They ceased wandering, moved from caves to villages of pit houses, and became farmers as well as hunters.

Over several hundred years, three distinct cultures emerged. In the east-central mountains and forests the **Mogollon** people hunted, gathered nuts and berries, farmed, and became the first Arizonans to make pottery. The **Anasazi**, descendants of archaic basket makers, inhabited the northern Plateau and built multi-leveled villages on high mesas and cliffs. Their villages, or pueblos, were often constructed around a central plaza and featured underground kivas for religious ceremonies.

In south-central Arizona's Salt and Gila River valleys, the **Hohokam** flourished, producing pottery, jewelry, and a political system which lasted for over 2,000 years. Their elaborate canal system stretched over 250 miles to irrigate fields of corn, beans, and cotton. As the three groups met, traded, and intermingled, the Salado, Patayan, Sinagua, and other subcultures developed.

The Great Disappearance

The prehistoric Indian cultures reached their zenith between A.D. 700 and the late 1200s in what has been called the **Great Pueblo period**. During this time they built elaborate apartment houses with as many as four stories and dozens of rooms.

By 1450, all of these cultures had completely disappeared. Droughts which lasted for several years, disease, invading enemies, and cultural assimilation into other tribes may have caused the disappearance. The remains of their villages dot the Arizona landscape. Many are preserved as National Monuments.

What's in a Name?

We don't know what prehistoric Native Americans called themselves. Anasazi is a Navajo word meaning "ancient ones." Hohokam means "those who have vanished," and comes from the Pima language. Archaeologists have given the name Mogollon, pronounced "MUGGY-own," to ancient tribes that inhabited the area around the Mogollon Rim.

Southwest Regional Office/NPS

The Anasazi built elaborate cliff dwellings at Tonto National Monument and other sites throughout the Southwest

One Person's Trash . . . Prehistoric people were terrible housekeepers. Many let their garbage and discards accumulate in heaps. Preserved in caves and pueblo rooms, and protected from decay by Arizona's arid climate, the refuse provides a treasure trove of information on foods they grew and ate and the tools they used. Pottery designs offer clues to differentiate between prehistoric cultures.

Ruins and Remains

1) Canyon de Chelly National Monument: Remains of almost all prehistoric Southwestern cultures are found in the Canyon's 300 prehistoric sites and 138 major ruins, dated A.D. 350–1300. *FYI:* Navajo Reservation; 602-674-5436.

2) Tonto National Monument: A self-guiding, half-mile trail leads to Salado cliff dwellings built around 1300. The visitor center displays some of the southwest's best-preserved prehistoric fabrics and vegetal material. *FYI:* AZ 88; 602-467-2241.

3) Montezuma Castle National Monument: The Aztec leader never saw this 20-room, five-story apartment house, built around A.D. 1250. One of the nation's best-preserved cliff dwellings, it contains original ceiling timbers and its builders' finger marks. *FYI:* INT. 17; 602-567-3322.

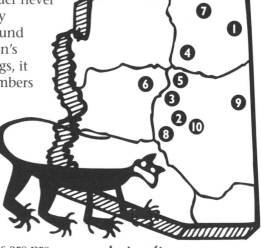

4) Wupatki National Monument: An open-air amphitheater, ball court, and over 800 homesites ranging from one-family dwellings to a three-story pueblo with 100-plus rooms are preserved in this prehistoric town. *FYI:* US 89; 602-527-3367.

Ancient Sites

5) Walnut Canyon National Monument: A steep trail with 185 feet of steps leads through an idyllic canyon and among 25 well-preserved cliff dwellings. The 300 Sinagua ruins on the rim and in the canyon date to about A.D. 1100. *FYI:* US 180; 602-526-3367.

6) Tuzigoot National Monument: This 110-room Sinagua pueblo flourished from A.D. 1100–1450 on a ridge overlooking the Verde River. A trail leads through over 100 rooms, and a museum exhibits pottery, textiles, stone weapons, and tools. *FYI:* AZ Alt 89; 602-634-5564.

7) Navajo National Monument: Arizona's largest prehistoric cliff dwelling site includes the state's biggest Anasazi ruin. Expect a strenuous day, with a five-mile trip to Betatakin or a tough eight-mile hike or horseback ride to Keet Seel. *FYI:* Tonalea; 602-672-2366.

8) Casa Grande: Was it a dwelling, lookout tower, ceremonial site, or astronomical observatory? Archaeologists are still debating its use.

Southwest Regional Office/NPS

Spectacular gorges protect ancient ruins at Canyon de Chelly

Hard Labor
Whether it was constructing a cliff dwelling or a canal, nothing was easy in prehistoric times. Rock, sand, and water had to be hauled up cliffs on primitive ladders to the dwelling. Water was carried a few quarts at a time in pitch-lined baskets or small pots. Digging a canal—sometimes over 15 feet deep—required an organized society using digging sticks to break the hard, dry earth. Trees for cross beams had to be floated or dragged by teams of men to building sites.

Most agree prehistoric architecture reached its zenith in this four-story structure built around A.D. 1300. *FYI:* AZ Alt. 287, Coolidge; 602-723-3172.

9) Casa Malpais: At one of the nation's largest prehistoric Mogollon communities, a 1.5-hour tour climbs 250 feet over a lava flow to a 120-room, three-story masonry pueblo. This major ceremonial center, built A.D. 1265–1380, contains rock art and one of the country's best-preserved kivas. *FYI:* Springerville; 602-333-5375.

10) Besh Ba Gowah Archaeological Park: Salado farmers lived in this 200-room pueblo from A.D. 1225–1400. Models, photographs, and museum exhibits interpret their life. *FYI:* 150 N. Pine, Globe; 602-425-0320.

The Amerind Foundation
Situated amidst spectacular rock formations, this museum contains one of the nation's finest collections of prehistoric and historic Indian artifacts. *FYI:* Texas Canyon; 602-586-3666.

Spanish and Mexican Rule, 1500–1848

In 1539, Franciscan Friar Fray Marcos and former slave Estevan ventured into Arizona searching for the fabled seven cities of Cibola. Estevan, wearing bells and brilliant feathers, convinced native tribes that he was a god—until he met the Zuni Indians, who didn't buy his act and promptly killed him. Fray Marcos retreated to Mexico City with a greatly exaggerated report of the area's wealth that led to the launching of the 1540 Coronado expedition.

Coronado spent two years in the southwest, harassing Indians and sending out expeditions to find the legendary cities. Instead of streets paved with gold and castles decorated with jewels, they found mud huts and stone villages. Coronado's assistant, Garcia Lopez de Cardenas, discovered the Grand Canyon. The 4,750-acre **Coronado National Memorial**, situated near the point where the expedition entered the United States, offers a spectacular view of Arizona and Mexico from 6,575-foot Montezuma Pass and Coronado Peak. *FYI:* Rural Route 2, Hereford; 602-366-5515.

In 1598, Juan de Oñate claimed Arizona for Spain. Missionaries followed, bringing Christianity, agriculture, and cattle. The first *presidio*, or fort, was established in 1752 at Tubac, the oldest European settlement in Arizona. **Tubac Presidio State Historic Park** includes an underground view of the fort's remains. *FYI:* 602-398-2252.

In 1775, Spain also built forts at Tucson and Presidio Santa de Terrentate. While Tucson became one of the oldest continuously inhabited cities in the country, Santa de Terrentate was abandoned after withstanding five years of Apache raids. A stone foundation and several adobe walls remain. *FYI:* Tombstone area; 602-457-2265.
San Xavier del Bac Mission: The White Dove of the Desert was founded by Jesuit Father Eusebio Francisco Kino in the 1700s.

Destroyed in a 1751 Indian uprising, it was rebuilt by Franciscan friars in 1768. It is the nation's oldest mission still serving Indians. Self-guided tours Monday through Saturday. *FYI:* Tohono O'odham Reservation; 602-294-2624.
Tumacacori National Historical Park: Father Kino started this mission

Tubac Presidio State Historic Park features an old-time newspaper print shop

Arizona State Parks

at the request of local Indians. Constructed 1796–1808, the structure was never completed, but was used as a church until 1828. The self-guided tour takes visitors through the church, cemetery, and mortuary. *FYI:* Tumacacori; 602-398-2341.

Eusebio Francisco Kino (1645–1711)
Many consider Father Kino Arizona's founder. During 25 years of exploration he traveled over 20,000 miles, proved that Baja California was not an island, and produced the first accurate maps of southern Arizona and northern Mexico. He also made the first astronomical observations in the American West, established 24 missions, and started Arizona's livestock industry by importing cattle.

Mexico Rules

When Mexico won its independence from Spain in 1821, Arizona became part of New Mexico Territory. The Spanish virtually abandoned Arizona, except for tiny garrisons at Tubac and Tucson. The next 26 years were marked by American-Mexican conflicts and territorial Indian warfare. When the Mexican-American War ended in 1848 with the signing of the Treaty of Guadalupe Hidalgo, all of Arizona north of the Gila River became United States property. The Gadsden Purchase of 1854 added land south of the river and established the current boundary between Arizona and Mexico.

Southwest Regional Office/NPS

Tumacacori was one of over 20 missions founded by Father Kino

The Mormon Battalion

Brigham Young offered to send a battalion to participate in the war against Mexico. The battalion was ordered to take Tucson and find a passable route through Arizona to California. Greatly outnumbered by the Mormons, Tucson Presidio surrendered on December 17, 1846, without a shot being fired. **Pipe Spring National Monument** was originally an 1870s Mormon tithing ranch. Surrounded by brilliant vermilion cliffs, it displays a fortress-like "Windsor Castle" home, and other buildings. *FYI:* Moccasin; 602-643-7105.

Territorial Days, 1850–1912

The Gadsden Purchase, mining, and the Civil War became key forces in propelling Arizona toward statehood. Along with them came ranchers, businessmen, army forts, Indian and land wars, con men, and gunfighters to write an indelible part of the history and legend of the American West.

Mining towns sprang up, said Mark Twain, wherever there was "a rumor and a hole in the ground." Fortunes were often made and sometimes lost overnight as mining ventures jumped from gold to silver to copper. In 1858, with the first big gold discovery, Gila City attracted 1,000 people, then quickly became a ghost town. By the 1880s, copper was king and boomtowns were born at Globe, Miami, Superior, Ajo, Jerome, and Ray.

One of the longest-lasting bonanzas was at **Bisbee**. Developed in the 1880s by Phelps Dodge Company, Bisbee's mines continued operating until the 1970s and produced over eight billion pounds of copper. Reminders of its glory days are the restored Brewery Gulch (a famous strip of saloons and gambling houses) and the Lavender Copper Mine's open pit. *FYI:* 602-432-5421

By the 1860s, cattle ranching, cotton and vegetable farms, and citrus orchards were thriving. In 1883, the Transcontinental Railroad accelerated growth by providing easier access to Arizona and a faster way to move products to markets.

National Archives and Records Administration

A game of faro at the Orient Saloon in Bisbee, circa 1900

Copper mining was the backbone of Bisbee's economy for nearly a century

Arizona Office of Tourism

Sharlot Hall Museum
The complex includes the original log cabin territorial Governor's "mansion," as well as other historic buildings. *FYI:* 415 Gurley, Prescott; 602-445-3122.

Who Was Bill Williams?
As a preacher, trapper, trader, and scout, Bill Williams (1787–1849) wandered from Missouri throughout the West. He was among the first Anglos to see California's Yosemite Valley and make an eastward crossing of the Sierra Nevada Mountains. Killed by Ute Indians, his memory lives in the name of an Arizona town, river, and mountain range.

Pleasant Valley's Unpleasant War
In 1887, the Tewksbury and Graham clans clashed in a sheep-herders-vs.-cattlemen feud that defied lawmen's efforts to restore peace. Five years later, when the shooting stopped, virtually the entire valley was involved. Over 30 people, including all the Grahams, were killed and are buried in Young's Cemetery. Zane Gray's novel *To the Last Man* dramatized the war.

Camel Caravans
Camels appeared to be the ideal beast of burden for the southwest desert. Imported by the U.S. government in the 1850s, they carried heavy loads, swam streams, and climbed snow-covered mountains. They also had nasty dispositions, stank, spit, bit, and kicked hard enough to kill a mule. Eventually they were turned loose and roamed the desert until they died. Near Quartzsite, a copper camel marks the grave of Syrian camel-driver and prospector Hi Jolly (Hadji Ali).

Santa Fe Railway

Prescott's railway station and staff were symbols of progress in the 1890s

Civil War in Arizona

Since many Arizona settlers were ex-Southerners, they voted to join the Confederacy. Although Arizona was claimed as a territory by both North and South, the Union prevailed when Congress created the Arizona Territory on February 24, 1863. A temporary capital at Fort Whipple soon gave way to a permanent one at Prescott.

In February 1862, Confederate cavalry arrived at Tucson and Union troops occupied Yuma. The two armies met at Picacho Peak in what has been called the Westernmost Battle of the Civil War. Before retreating to Tucson, the Confederates killed and captured a total of six Union soldiers.

Picacho Peak State Park: This 3,400-acre park on the slopes of a volcanic pinnacle encompasses the battle site. It offers colorful desert camping, picnicking, and some of the biggest, best, and brightest springtime wildflower displays. *FYI:* I-10. 602-466-3183.

The Baron of Arizona

James Addison Reavis concocted an elaborate scheme to obtain deeds to vast land grants that included Phoenix and an area larger than Connecticut and Delaware combined. The former mule-skinner spent years traveling Mexico and Arizona altering public records to support his claim, and petitioned the U.S. government to give him the deeds. Many landowners, including corporations, retained their property by paying his asking price.

Until the fraud was exposed and he was sent to prison, the self-proclaimed Baron of Arizona lived in grand style with homes in Arizona, St. Louis, Washington, Mexico, and Madrid.

Indian Wars

Dedicated leaders and a large Indian population capable of retreating into impenetrable mountains and canyons gave Arizona an unmatched history of Indian warfare.

Navajos battled Spanish and U.S. troops for 150 years before Kit Carson defeated them at Canyon de Chelly. Using rival tribes, he captured 8,000 Navajos and marched them on the Long Walk to captivity in eastern New Mexico.

Cochise and Geronimo continued resisting until 1886 by leading Apache raids throughout southeastern Arizona.

Apache Pass: In 1862, Cochise stopped the Butterfield Overland Mail and fought one of Arizona's largest Indian battles here. Geronimo surrendered nearby. A 1.5-mile trail leads to the adobe ruins of Old Fort Bowie, which was established in 1862 to secure Apache Pass. It was often at the center of confrontations between the Army and Apaches. *FYI:* I-10; 602-847-2500.

Cochise Stronghold Canyon: For 15 years Cochise and 250 warriors used these beautiful wooded pinnacles in the Dragoon Mountains as a base for raids on the surrounding country-

Kit Carson, friend—then foe—of the Navajos

side. *FYI:* 30 miles SW of Willcox; 602-670-6483.

Chiricahua National Monument: A scenic drive and hiking trails lead through spectacular rocky crags and spires that were the ancestral home of Cochise and the Chiricahua Apaches. *FYI:* Willcox; 602-824-3560.

Apache Leap: According to legend, 75 Apache warriors jumped to their deaths from this cliff rather than surrender to the U.S. Cavalry. *FYI:* US 60; 602-425-4495.

Fort Verde State Historic Park: Visitors can tour four original buildings from the 1865 fort which served as a base for military action against the Apaches. *FYI:* Camp Verde; 602-567-3275.

Fort Huachuca: The nation's only remaining active cavalry post offers Apache War exhibits and narrated stagecoach-ride tours of the historic post area and cemetery. *FYI:* Fort Huachuca; 602-458-6940.

"The Long Walk" of 1863

Statehood

Although Arizona statehood bills were introduced as early as 1892, Congressional authorization did not come until 1912. When President William Howard Taft signed the proclamation on February 14, Arizona became the 48th and last state in the continental U.S.

At times there was more turmoil than love in the Valentine State. Pancho Villa's threat to attack Nogales, Arizona, and blow up the border barricades brought 10,000 U.S. troops to the area. They opened fire and killed many Mexicans. A 1918 shooting of a Mexican smuggler by U.S. Customs guards precipitated a conflict resulting in 32 American and 70 to 80 Mexican casualties.

Both World Wars fostered increased demands for Arizona's copper, cattle, and cotton. World War II saw bustling aircraft factories, General George Patton drilling ground troops in the desert, and the Army Air Corps training pilots in the clear, sunny skies. After the war, many servicemen returned to raise families and enjoy the natural and constructed attractions.

Arizona State Capital Museum: This National Register site, which served as the capitol of both the Arizona Territory and the State, has been restored to its 1912 appearance. You can step into the offices of the Governor and Secretary of State, and the House and Senate chambers. *FYI:* 1700 W. Washington, Phoenix; 602-542-4581.

Champlin Fighter Museum: Displays the world's first combat aircraft (1911), a Fokker Dr-l triplane, the extremely rare German Messerschmitt 109, P-51 Mustangs, and other World War I and II aircraft—from the obscure to the famous. Falcon Field, Mesa. *FYI:* Falcon Field, Mesa; 602-830-4540.

National Archives and Records Administration

Theodore Roosevelt presiding at the dedication ceremony of Roosevelt Dam, 1911

Pima Air Museum: The world's largest privately funded air museum covers all military services and displays many private and commercial planes, with over 180 aircraft, from the *Wright Flyer* to the *SR-71 Blackbird*. *FYI:* 6000 E. Valencia, Tucson; 602-574-9658.

Theodore Roosevelt Dam: The world's highest masonry dam, completed in 1911, was the first federal reclamation project. It stands 275 feet high and forms a lake 25 miles long. Theodore Roosevelt called it "the most awe-inspiring and most sublimely beautiful panorama nature has ever created." *FYI: AZ 188.*

Glory Hole Antiques on historic Route 66 in Oatman

Photo courtesy of Bureau of Land Management

Route 66

From 1926 through 1984, U.S. 66 was a major American east-west thoroughfare. Immortalized by John Steinbeck in *The Grapes of Wrath*, Route 66 j1is often called Adventure's Highway, America's Main Street, and The Mother Road.

Although largely replaced by Interstate 40 in Arizona, the 42-mile segment of original Route 66 from McConnico to Golden Shores has been designated a Bureau of Land Management Back Country Byway. The scenic route's attractions include a historic spring, gas station, and camping area. It also meanders past the Tri-State Overlook with views of Arizona, California, and Nevada; Oatman ghost town; and Gold Road townsite remnants. Route 66 is not recommended for vehicles over 40 feet long.

The Zimmerman Telegram

This infamous telegram was sent by Germany to Mexico. In return for its alliance, Germany hinted that it would help Mexico ". . . reconquer the lost territory in Texas, New Mexico, and Arizona." Intercepted and decoded by the British, the message infuriated Arizonans, who enlisted in droves and hastened America's entry into World War I.

Modern Times

After World War II, it seemed everyone discovered Arizona. Between 1940 and 1970 the state's population tripled, then doubled during the 1970s and 1980s. By 1990, there were 3.8 million people living in Arizona.

People from around the world mix business and pleasure at Arizona's deluxe hotels and resorts

Hordes of senior citizens became permanent residents. Attracted by the hospitable climate and year-round recreation opportunities, another 20 million people vacationed in Arizona each year. Resorts and retirement communities rose in the desert, providing elegant retreats for the golden years and havens from the nation's harsh winters. Arizona also did booming business in conventions, conferences, and retreats. So many people came and went in 1991 that traffic into and out of Phoenix's Sky Harbor Airport had a $32-million-a-day impact! Tourism and service industries provided over 55 percent of the jobs, and visitors contributed about $7 billion annually to the local economy.

The Industrial Complex

Business and industry also thrived in Arizona. Electrical and transportation equipment manufacturing became leading industries, and other organizations found it an ideal spot for making computers, electronic components, aerospace equipment, and military operations. At one time there were 18 Titan ballistic missiles sites strategically placed around the Tucson basin. At the **Titan II Missile Museum**, a deactivated site, visitors can descend into the missile silo, step into the launch control center, and watch monitoring and countdown procedures. *FYI:* I-19, Green Valley; 602-791-2929.

Mixing business with pleasure turned Arizona into one of the nation's leading playgrounds.

Resorts and Retirement Centers

☞ **Rio Rico Resort and Country Club:** This stylish golf, tennis, and conference resort perches high atop a mesa a few miles north of Nogales. *FYI:* I-19, Rio Rico; 602-281-1901.

☞ **Tubac Golf Resort:** Guests tee off on a historic ranch with nature trails and nearby bird-watching sanctuaries. *FYI:* Tubac; 602-398-9261.

☞ **Sunrise Park Resort:** Arizona's premier ski resort offers three mountains, and summer biking, hiking and fishing. *FYI:* McNary; 602-735-7676.

☞ **Arizona Inn:** This 1930s National Register hotel overlooks 14 acres of lawn and gardens, and also offers tennis and swimming. *FYI:* Tucson; 602-325-1541.

☞ **Canyon Ranch Spa:** Along with deluxe accommodations and gourmet cuisine, the award-winning spa features fitness classes, hiking, biking, swimming, racquet sports, and therapeutic body treatments. *FYI:* Tucson; 602-749-9000.

☞ **Del Webb's Sun City Tucson:** This award-winning adult community is built around a 1,000-acre master plan, 11 model homes, and a $6,000,000 recreation center. *FYI:* Tucson; 602-825-5900.

☞ **Fairfield Green Valley:** This planned retirement community is situated around five golf courses with over $8 million in recreational amenities. *FYI:* Green Valley; 602-791-2900.

Prominent Arizonans

Barry Goldwater. When he was born in 1909, Arizona was still a territory. As a U.S. senator, Barry Goldwater was elected five times and served a total of 30 years. He was the 1964 Republican presidential candidate, but lost to Lyndon Johnson.

Judge Lorna Lockwood. In 1965 she became the nation's first woman to head a state supreme court.

Sandra Day O'Connor. In 1981 she became the first woman appointed to the U.S. Supreme Court.

National Geographic Society

Supreme Court Justice Sandra Day O'Connor

THE NATURAL WORLD

Building the Earth

Arizona's geologic history has been marked by the rise of mountains and the spread of deserts. About 500 million years ago, while much of the world was high and dry, Arizona lay at the bottom of an ocean. Waters teemed with ancient crab-like creatures and clams. After they died their shells gradually became limestone, which has served as a building material ever since.

Over centuries, the land slowly rose and seas drained. As the water receded, the earth's crust hardened; earthquakes shook the land; volcanoes spouted hot ash and lava; and uplifting created mountains. About 63 million years ago, the seas rolled in one last time, covering the land with sand dunes.

Through the centuries water and wind eroded the surface, forming canyons, mesas, and buttes. Plateaus rose in northern Arizona, and faulting created basins in the south. The Colorado River shifted course, eroding new channels and canyons.

The moving and shaking left a state which slopes from northeast to southwest. By two million years ago the landscape looked much as it does today.

National Archives and Records Administration

Fort Thomas officers and guests lunch under a giant cactus, 1886. The saguaro is the signature plant of the Sonoran desert.

Geographical Regions

The southwest basin and range terrain is mostly desert, with sparse vegetation, rolling hills, and craggy, barren mountains rising abruptly from its level floor. Green mountains and beautiful valleys curve from the eastern border northward through central Arizona, and are cut by the 200-mile-long sheer cliff of the Mogollon Rim, which rises to 7,500 feet. The nation's largest stand of ponderosa pine fills mountainsides and valleys. Above the rim, the snow-clad San Francisco Peaks rise to 12,670 feet. In the northeast corner, the Colorado Plateau has been carved into deserts, mesas, stately spires, and the awe-inspiring Grand Canyon.

Four Deserts

Four deserts, each with distinct climate, biology, and scenery, make up between half and two-thirds of Arizona.

The beautiful, varied, southern **Sonoran desert** stretches south into Mexico. Split by the Gila and Salt rivers, it has at least 12 mountains and ranges scattered across its plains, and is home to pack rats, coatimundi, javelina, Gila monsters, and over 300 species of birds.

A tip of the **Chihuahuan desert** edges into southeastern Arizona. Although it receives 8 to 10 inches of rain per year, most of it is a flat wasteland. Willcox Playa appears to be a vast shimmering lake but is a permanent mirage covering a 50-square-mile basin.

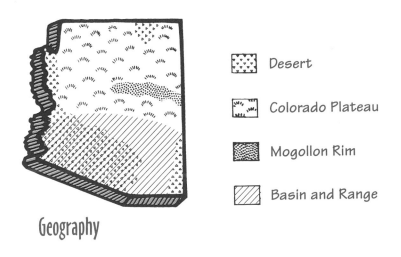

Desert

Colorado Plateau

Mogollon Rim

Basin and Range

Geography

The **Great Basin desert** dips into the northeast corner, covering the Colorado Plateau and the Navajo Indian Reservation. It is a land of deep canyons, and sandstone skylines punctuated by cliffs, mesas, and spires.

Soft, fluid dunes of the **Mojave desert** spread across the northwestern edge. No other North American desert is as dry, hot, inhospitable, and unforgiving. Although the area receives only about 4.5 inches of rain per year, the creosote bush thrives in the Mojave. It lives up to 11,000 years, making it the oldest living thing on earth. The Joshua tree, which lives as long as 500 years, is the Mojave's signature plant, much as the saguaro is in the Sonoran desert.

National Parks

It has been called the Big Ditch, the grandest of canyons, and one of the wonders of the world. By whatever name, the **Grand Canyon**'s immensity is overwhelming, the majesty of its seemingly infinite rock formations is awe-inspiring, and its colorful land-scape with subtle shades of purple, red, yellow, and green defies the imagination.

South Rim of the Grand Canyon

Arizona Office of Tourism

Although some of its rocks are approximately two billion years old, the canyon was born in the last five to six million years. Shaped by land-slides, sand, and the elements, its exposed walls contain the history of the earth's formation (beginning with the original crust), and of life on earth, from the first crabs to the latest mammals. Mingling with today's scenery are 75 species of mammals, 50 reptiles and amphibians, and over 300 birds.

Counting all its twists and turns, the canyon meanders 277 miles and is 600 feet to 18 miles wide. It's average depth is one mile. At an elevation of 8,200 feet the North Rim is about 1,000 feet higher than the South Rim.

Two drives along the South Rim provide an easy introduction for automobile travelers. The North Rim Drive offers spectacular vistas from Cape Royal, Point Imperial, and across-the-Canyon views of the Painted Desert. While it's only 10 miles from rim to rim, by car they're 215 miles apart. To hike between them is a

tough three-day trek. For less exertion and more fun, make reservations a year in advance and take a mule trip into the canyon. Approximately 20 operators also tour the canyon on Colorado River raft and boat trips lasting from a few days to three weeks. *FYI:* Grand Canyon National Park; 602-638-7888.

John Wesley Powell (1834–1903)

In 1869, John Wesley Powell and a nine-man crew made the first journey through the Grand Canyon of the Colorado River. A man of many talents, Powell was a Harvard-educated college professor, geologist, botanist, and Civil War major who lost an arm at Shiloh. He also explored Colorado's mountains, helped establish the U.S. Geological Survey, and made a second trip through the Grand Canyon in 1871.

John Wesley Powell

Grand Canyon National Park

Petrified Forest

About 225 million years ago, northeastern Arizona was covered with lush ferns, cycads, and towering trees similar to sequoias and pines. Giant amphibians feasted on fish and the first dinosaurs. When trees and animals died, they were washed into a flood plain and covered by silt, mud, and volcanic ash which cut off oxygen and slowed decay. Over the centuries silica from groundwater seeped through the logs, crystallized into quartz, and turned the trees into "petrified" wood.

This National Park contains the world's largest concentration of petrified wood. Some of North America's oldest dinosaur fossils were found here, along with over 8,000 years of Indian sites. A 28-mile road leads to several "forests" of broken agate and jasper logs, splashed with the bright reds, yellows, greens, and blues wrought by iron oxide. Along the rim of the Painted Desert iron oxide has stained the undulating mounds, hills, and rocks in pink, orange, purple, red, and blue-gray. Camping, hiking. *FYI:* Petrified Forest; 602-524-6228.

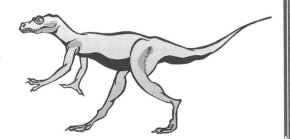

Parks, Monuments, and Natural Attractions

1) Chiricahua National Monument: Approximately 25,000 years ago, white-hot ash from a nearby caldera blanketed this area in a 2,000-foot layer. Fused layers were uplifted, creating mountains which were eroded by wind, water, and ice. Called the "Wonderland of Rocks" they are a spectacular wilderness of stony crags, spires, natural bridges, grottos, and balanced rocks. Scenic drives, hiking, camping. *FYI:* Willcox; 602-824-3560.

2) Colossal Cave: The cave is believed to be the world's largest dry limestone cavern, and even today parts remain unexplored. A 40-minute guided tour covers the geology and involves many steps. *FYI:* 22 miles east of Tucson; 602 791-7677.

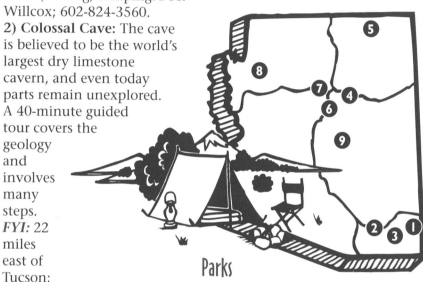

Parks

3) Karchner Caverns State Park: The infinite artistry of water is displayed in this 2.5-mile-long cavern where virtually every cave formation grows. Only recently discovered, it's scheduled to open in 1995. *FYI:* 16 miles south of Benson; 602-542-4174.

Southwest Regional Office/NPS

Sunset Crater

4) Meteor Crater: About 50,000 years ago a huge meteor struck the earth at nearly 45,000 miles per hour, leaving a hole 570 feet deep and about a mile across. Astronauts trained on its slopes for moon landings, and the site's Astronaut Hall of

Fame displays a space capsule. *FYI:* Off AR 99, 35 miles east of Flagstaff.

5) Monument Valley: This fantasyland of wide-open spaces, buttes, spires, arches, and flat desert was once a solid sandstone plateau as high as some of its 1,000-foot pinnacles. While a 14-mile drive on marked roads takes you to some of the best-known landmarks, a guided jeep tour gets you off the beaten path and into the backcountry. *FYI:* Window Rock; 602-871-6647.

6) Oak Creek Canyon: This magnificent 16-mile-long gorge includes some of Arizona's most spectacular scenery: forests, Oak Creek's quiet pools and rushing rapids, and red-rock formations that change color during the day and the seasons. Six National Forest campgrounds. *FYI:* Sedona; 606-282-7722.

7) San Francisco Peaks: Sometime between 2.8 million and 200,000 years ago, San Francisco Peak erupted and part of its 15,000-foot cone collapsed into a magma chamber. Glaciers smoothed the lowlands and left the volcano with four summits. Humphreys Peak, at 12,670 feet—Arizona's highest point—is a primary winter sports area, also offering summer hiking trails, chairlift rides, and magnificent wildflower displays. *FYI:* US 89, Flagstaff; 602-779-1951.

8) Sunset Crater National Monument: Sunset Crater erupted in A.D. 1064, spewing ash and lava over 800 square miles and leaving a symmetrical cone 1,000 feet high, plus cinder cones, lava flows, and ice caves. In its final eruption around A.D. 1250, red and yellow oxidized iron and sulfur fell onto the rim as a permanent "sunset." *FYI:* US 89; 602-556-7042.

9) Tonto Natural Bridge State Park: The world's largest travertine bridge, formed by mineral deposits from the waters of natural springs, is 400 feet wide, 283 feet high, and spans a 150-foot-wide canyon. A small waterfall cascades over the top of the arch. There are viewpoints at the top and from trails in the fern-draped, spring-fed canyon. *FYI:* Payson; 602-476-4202.

Phoenix Convention Bureau

Jeep tours provide opportunities to see the back country of Monument Valley, Sedona, the Navajo Reservation and other parts of Arizona

Weathering the Weather

Mark Twain said "Arizona's temperature remains at a constant 120 degrees in the shade, except when it varies and goes higher." Mark said a lot of things that weren't true, and that was one of them.

Temperatures contrast greatly between summer and winter, day and night, and mountains and desert. Although the sun shines more than 80 percent of the time, the combination of sunshine, low humidity, and crystal-clear air has become one of Arizona's greatest assets. In summer the lower regions are almost universally hot, but the mountains are cool and inviting. In the southern desert summer, thermometers often zoom over 100° Fahrenheit then drop to the 70s and 80s at night. High-country regions range from 70° to 80° in summer. The state's average daytime temperature in July is 80°, while evenings frequently drop to the 50s.

While winter temperatures dip below zero in the mountains, deserts may not drop below freezing for years. Winter temperatures average in the 50s in the low desert and the 20s to 30s in the mountains.

Arizona receives most of its rain from December through February and July through August. Its average precipitation is 13.69 inches. The line of demarcation between rainstorms and dry weather is so marked that some insist you can wash your hands in the rain without getting your cuffs wet.

Average Arizona Temperatures

City	Flagstaff	Grand Canyon	Phoenix	Tucson
Winter	42° - 15°	43° - 20°	66° - 38°	65° - 38°
Spring	56° - 26°	60° - 31°	83° - 51°	80° - 50°
Summer	77° - 46°	81° - 50°	106° - 80°	104° - 78°
Fall	61° - 31°	63° - 36°	86° - 56°	83° - 56°

Temperature Trivia

☛ The highest temperature ever recorded in Arizona was 127°F on July 7, 1905 at Parker.

☛ Arizona's lowest temperature of – 40°F was recorded on January 7, 1971 at Hawley Lake.

Flora and Fauna

The diversity of topography and climate provide rich habitats for plants and animals. In fact, on a hike from Arizona's lowest to highest point you could encounter the same plants, animals, and climatic changes that you would see on a walk from Mexico to Canada!

Coyotes are abundant in Arizona

Wildlife and Plant Trivia

☛ Arizona's largest lizard, the Gila monster, is one of the world's two poisonous lizards and the only one found in the United States.

☛ The kangaroo rat can live its entire life without drinking water, obtaining moisture through a chemical process from digesting food.

☛ A member of the goat family, the pronghorn has a four-part stomach that acts as a fermentation vat. Capable of running 60 miles per hour for short bursts, this is North America's fastest mammal.

☛ When flutings on the barrel cactus contract, the whole plant bends to the south, forming a kind of compass.

☛ The century plant does not actually live 100 years. It grows slowly until the flowering stem appears, then may grow as rapidly as 12 inches in 24 hours.

☛ Arizona trout, Grand Canyon rattlesnakes, and Kaibab squirrels are found only in Arizona.

Arizona's native birds range from comical roadrunners, wild turkeys, and Arizona and Gila woodpeckers to colorful cardinals. Sandhill cranes, thick-billed parrots from Mexico, and a variety of flycatchers migrate in and out.

Wildlife varies from the common coyote, that symbol of the American West, to bobcats, ocelots, desert fox, raccoons, ringtail cats, and coatimundis. Herds of wild horses and burros, descended from domestic stock, roam the canyons and backcountry.

The Gila monster is one of the many distinctive animals native to the region

Desert Gardens

Arizona's common desert plants include ironwood, paloverde, and ocotillo, which brighten spring landscapes, along with brittle bush, cliff rose, and hummingbird bush. In forests and higher elevations, look for ponderosa pine, Douglas and white fir, Engelmann spruce, aspen, Arizona cypress, piñon pine, juniper, walnut, and sycamore.

Saguaro National Monument: While the monument was established to preserve forests of saguaro cactus, at least six distinct biological communities exist within the boundaries of its two sections. The Rincon Mountain unit, east of Tucson, is a patchwork of ocotillo, catclaw, prickly pear, barrel, saguaro, and four varieties of cholla cactus. The Tucson Mountain District, west of the city, contains the nation's finest stand of saguaros and ironwood. Extending up a wild jumble of mountains dominated by 4,687-foot-high Wasson Peak, it contains over 600 species of plants, 200 bird species, and 50 reptiles. Hiking trails and scenic drives lead through both units. *FYI:* 3693 Old Spanish Trail, Tucson; 602-670-6680.

Organ Pipe Cactus National Monument: Three deserts meet and merge at the monument, intermingling their flora and fauna. Twenty-six varieties of cactus grow here, along with many rare Mexican plants. It is the only spot where the organ-pipe, the elephant tree, and the "bearded" senita exist in the same area. Called the Aristocrat of the American Desert, the organ-pipe has as many as 50 tubular arms shooting up to heights of 25 to 50 feet. While organ pipes are common in Mexico, this monument is the only place in America where they thrive. The stark mountains, razorback ridges, rocky canyons, and dry washes are also home to the endangered Sonoran pronghorn, mountain lions, bobcats, grey wolves, and the only

Arizona Office of Tourism

The paloverde is the official state tree

species of javelina in the United States. March through June is the best time to see the cactus in bloom. *FYI:* Ajo; 602-387-6849.

Boyce Thompson Arboretum: Trails lead through plants from arid lands around the world. Scientists conduct research on the site, and special events, lectures, and workshops are offered throughout the year. The buildings are listed on the National Register of Historic Sites. *FYI:* Superior; 602-689-2723.

Arizona-Sonora Desert Museum: A stroll through the outdoor museum offers all the advantages—and none of the dangers—of a real walk in the desert. The *New York Times* called it the most distinctive zoo in the United States. Among the more than 200 animals and 400 plants are everything from minuscule centipedes, tarantulas, and scorpions, to San Esteban Island chuckwallas, Gila monsters, bobcats, prairie dogs, and rattlesnakes. River otters cavort in a riparian habitat while Mexican wolves, black bear, and mountain lions move through oak-pine woodlands. Over 300 birds common to the Sonoran Desert can be seen in the walk-through aviaries. *FYI:* Tucson Mountain Park; 602-883-2702.

A butterfly alights on a brightly colored bougainvillea

Arizona Office of Tourism

Desert Botanical Garden: Over 20,000 plants from deserts around the world have been transplanted here. A three-acre Southwest section offers a bit of history with buildings and prehistoric ruins, and

a peek at Sonoran desert environments on a trail leading past a desert stream and through a stand of saguaros, into mesquite and upland chaparral. *FYI:* Phoenix; 602-941-1225.

Using the Land

Chances are some of the clothes you wear, the copper in your electrical wires, and the silver in your money came from Arizona.

Arizona is a major beef-producing state where cowboys still work the range

Mining produces about $1.5 billion per year, or 3 percent of the gross state product. By the 1980s Arizona led the nation in total production of all metals except iron. The leading producer of copper since 1888, it still mines more of that metal than all 49 other states combined. In the smelting process, copper ore yields gold, molybdenum, and silver. Zinc, lead, and uranium are also mined. Other minerals whose gemstone quality contributes significantly to the state's economy are turquoise, peridot, amethyst, precious opal, and fire agate.

The Globe-Miami area ranks among the west's great historic mining districts. A self-driving auto tour on US 60 between Globe and Miami takes visitors to several open-pit and underground sites, some still active, and past historic copper mines, crushers, and smelters. *FYI:* 602-338-8983.

Agriculture accounts for 1 percent of the gross state product. Thanks to its long growing season, Arizona produces three cotton crops per year—and no state grows more per acre. Seventy percent of the land is still used for grazing cattle. While most of the wide open range has been fenced and Herefords have replaced the pioneers' longhorns, in some areas it's still possible to see cattle drives and working cowboys on horseback.

Circa 1907, a cowboy and his horse pause for a drink of water, Arizona's most precious resource

Endangered Species

The influx of people, agriculture, and industry has not come without its price. Today, water is Arizona's most precious resource. The state uses more water than is generated by rain or snow runoff and in places the earth has actually sunk as much as 12 feet due to water table depletion.

Heavy land use has also placed severe pressure on wildlife. Arizona's endangered species include:

Fish: of 35 species of fish native to Arizona, 25 are threatened because dams or other building projects are destroying or altering streams. Among them are the Yaqui catfish, bonytail chub, loach minnow, desert pupfish, Little Colorado spinedance, Colorado squawfish, Gila topminnow, Apache trout.

Mammals: Sandborn's long-nosed bat, jaguar, Mt. Graham red squirrel, Hualapai Mexican vole.

Birds: masked bobwhite quail, Audubon's crested caracara, thick-billed parrot, wood stork.

Reptiles: desert tortoise.

Plants: Arizona agave, Cochise pincushion cactus, Arizona hedgehog cactus, Tumamoc globeberry, Navajo sedge, Arizona cliff rose.

Special Events
While Quartzsite's year-round population is about 3,500, it swells to 250,000 on the first weekend in February, during the **Quartzsite Pow Wow**. While over 80 percent of the displays are strictly gems and minerals, the event also features entertainment, giant flea markets, and other activities. *FYI:* 602-927-6325.

The **Tucson Gem and Mineral Show** caters to amateur and professional gem and mineral collectors, artisans, and the public with dealers, museum exhibits, and lectures and seminars on earth sciences. *FYI:* 602-322-5773.

CULTURES

Native Americans

Arizona's ethnic mix is linked directly to its Indian cultures and its settlement by Spain and Mexico. Today one-seventh of all of North America's Indians live in Arizona. Approximately 16 percent of Arizona's population is of either Spanish or Mexican descent.

About 160,000 members of 14 Indian tribes live on 20 reservations, covering over 19,000,000 acres. The reservation population and area are the largest in the nation. Many tribes have retained much of their tribal life and customs. Dances and other religious ceremonies mark important life events such as births, deaths, planting, and harvest, and are part of the fabric of daily life.

Ceremonial dances reflect centuries-old Native American traditions

Some, such as the Hopi and Pima, trace their ancestry to the prehistoric cliff-dwelling Anasazi and the canal-building Hohokam. The Apache and Navajo arrived in Arizona from southern Canada between A.D. 1200 and 1300. Others, such as the Yaqui, migrated northward from Mexico.

Cochise and Geronimo

Undoubtedly the two most famous of Arizona's Native Americans were Cochise and Geronimo. Both were leaders of the Chiricahua Apaches.

Although he conducted raids into Mexico from his Chiricahua Mountain homeland, **Cochise** maintained peaceful reign for several years. He allowed the Overland Stage to cross Apache lands and to build stations along the route.

The peaceful relations ended in 1861 when a group of Apaches raided a ranch and abducted a child. Cochise and five others were arrested. Although they denied knowledge of the crime, one Apache was shot and four were hanged. Cochise escaped and, vowing revenge, began ten years of savage warfare against settlers. With a small band of warriors, he successfully held off the U.S. Army and stopped Overland Stage runs.

Cochise lived in his homelands until his death. His tribe buried him in the Chiricahua Mountains and rode their ponies over the grave so that it could never be found.

After Cochise's death, **Geronimo** assumed lead-

National Archives and Records Administration

Geronimo and other Apache Indian prisoners on their way to exile in Florida, via the Southern Pacific Railway

ership of the tribe. His name, given to him by the Spanish, means "one who yawns." A controversial figure even in his own tribe, Geronimo's hatred of whites stemmed from the massacre of his mother, wife, and children by Mexican troops. Fiercely independent and determined to maintain his people's freedom, he waged brutal warfare against military and settlers until 1884. After escaping several times from the San Carlos reservation, he was defeated at Arizona's Skeleton Canyon, and exiled to Florida. Denied permission from the U.S. government to spend his last days in his beloved homeland, Geronimo died at Fort Sill, Oklahoma, in 1909 at age 80.

Do's and Don'ts

Each Native American tribe has a unique history and culture, as well as individual customs and regulations. At many reservations you can watch craftspeople creating fine weaving, pottery, and jewelry, and purchase arts and crafts directly from the artisans. But expect some restrictions. Some tribes do not allow tape-recording, videotaping, or photographing of tribal dances. Others may have sites or ceremonies that are off-limits to visitors. Do not venture off designated paths or enter private buildings without an invitation. Respect these traditions, and when in doubt, *ask questions*.

Arizona Native American Arts and Crafts

Reservation	Known For
Ak-Chin	Basketry
Camp Verde	Basketry
Cocopah East and West	Beadwork, gourd rattles, ribbon shirts, ribbon dresses
Colorado River	Basketry, beadwork, Indian motif wall clocks
Fort Apache	Burden baskets, beadwork
Fort McDowell	Basketry
Fort Mojave	Basketry, beadwork
Fort Yuma	Beadwork
Gila River	Pima basketry, Maricopa pottery
Havasupai	Basketry, beadwork
Hopi	Kachina dolls, polychrome pottery, basketry, jewelry, sand paintings
Hualapai	Basketry, dolls
Kaibab-Paiute	Coiled, shallow wedding baskets; leather bead work
Navajo	Blankets, rugs, tapestries, silverwork, sand paintings
Pascua-Yaqui	Children's cultural paintings, deer dance statues
Salt River	Basketry, pottery
San Carlos	Peridot jewelry, basketry, beadwork
Tohono O'Odham	Kiaha weaving, blankets, tapestry, silver crafts
Tonto Apache	Basketry, beadwork
Yavapai-Prescott	Basketry

Indian Reservations

1) Ak-Chin: The lush 21,840-acre desert is home to about 625 Tohono O'Odham Indians and the tribe's cotton farm. Visitors are welcome at the St. Francis Church Feast (October 4), which features local foods, and at the tribal election and barbecue on the second Saturday in January. *FYI:* Ak-Chin Indian Community, 42507 Peters & Mall Rd., Maricopa; 602-568-2227.

2) Camp Verde: Four separate communities in the Coconino National Forest became a reservation in 1871 by President Grant's order. The Apache Information Center houses a Tribal Museum with arts and crafts; the Verde River offers fishing and rafting. *FYI:* Camp Verde; 602-567-3649.

3) Cocopah East and West: About 600 Cocopahs, descended from Yumans that migrated from Baja California, live on three sections of the 6,000-acre reservation. Heritage Art Museum displays outstanding beadwork and native dress collections, and traditional tribal implements ranging from farming tools to hunting and recreational equipment. *FYI:* Somerton; 602-627-2102.

4) Colorado River: Established in 1865, the reservation straddles the Colorado River, California, and Arizona. Traditionally the Mojaves' home, its residents also include Chemehuevi, Hopi, and Navajos. The fertile bottomland yields a variety of crops and provides access to 100 miles of river recreation. Speedboat races have made Lake Moovala famous. Annual events include the Parker Enduro Boat Race, Indian Days Celebration and Rodeo, and a seven-mile Colorado River Inner-tube Race. *FYI:* Parker; 602-669-9211.

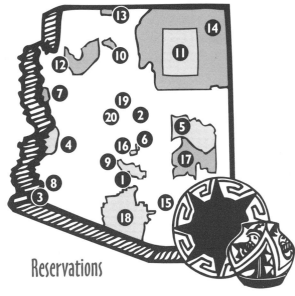

Reservations

5) Fort Apache: This is a 1.6-million-acre major recreation area with 25 lakes, 420 miles of trout streams, and numerous developed campgrounds, spread through desert foothills and some of Arizona's highest mountains. Tribally owned and operated Apache Sunrise Resort offers prime skiing. Visitors can see traditional Apache ceremonies at the tribal headquarters in Whiteriver, and many original buildings at Theodore Roosevelt Indian School. Fort Apache, on the school grounds, includes General George Crook's log cabin, which displays Indian, pioneer, and military relics. *FYI:* Whiteriver; 602-338-4346.

6) Fort McDowell: Now a suburb of Phoenix, Fort McDowell was a major military outpost from 1865 to 1890. The 24,680 acres of cottonwood-lined Verde River and cactus-studded desert were deeded to the Yavapai and Mojave-Apaches in 1903 by President Theodore Roosevelt. Its 630 residents manufacture Jojoba Bean Oil, a natural cosmetic used in hair and facial products. *FYI:* Fountain Hills; 602-990-0995.

7) Fort Mojave: Situated in Arizona, California, and Nevada, the reservation offers Colorado River fishing and bird hunting. Once the most warlike of all Yuman tribes, the Mojaves generally fought to the death when outnumbered. Mojave language and traditions are still used, including a Cry House where bodies of the dead are brought for tributes and grieving before cremation. *FYI:* AZ 95; 619-326-4591.

The Hopis' First Mesa, near Polacca

Southwest Regional Office/NPS

8) Fort Yuma: Established in 1884, the 44,400-acre reservation encompasses various buildings of Fort Yuma and St. Thomas Mission, built around 1858. Straddling the Colorado River and the Arizona/California border, it is rich in petroglyphs, geoglyphs, potholes, and other geological phenomena. *FYI:* Yuma; 619-572-0487.

9) Gila River: Arizona's oldest Indian reservation dates to 1859 and is home to 12,000 Pima and Maricopas. The Gila River Arts and Crafts Center sells Indian products from 19 tribes. Heritage Park displays represent all area tribes. *FYI:* Sacaton; 602-963-4323.

10) Havasupai: Situated at the bottom of 3,000-foot-deep Havasu Canyon, amid sparkling waterfalls and towering plateaus, the reservation can be reached via an 8-mile hike or mule ride to Supai Village. It is the last place in the United States where mail is still delivered by mule. Discovered by Spanish explorers, the tribe's 450 members still maintain many of their traditions. Peach trees, flowering orchards, and turquoise pools add to the idyllic scene. Limited overnight accommodations, campground, restaurants. *FYI:* Supai; 602-448-2961.

11) Hopi: Because their enemies were many and the Hopis were few, they withdrew to high mesas that rise dramatically from the colorful desert. The first Europeans found them living in pueblos and raising squash, corn, and beans. Oraibi Village, built around 1100, is one of the oldest continuously inhabited towns in the United States. The 1.5-million-acre reservation, created in 1882, is surrounded by Navajo lands. Most of the 9,000 Hopis live in 12 villages on three mesas. While oil and coal deposits provide some revenue, many Hopis farm the terraced fields. The reservation often pulses with rhythms of ceremonies and dances unchanged for generations. Liquor, cameras, sound recorders, and sketch pads are prohibited. Artwork and crafts are sold at the Hopi Cultural Center on Second Mesa. *FYI:* AZ 264; 602-743-2401.

12) Hualapai: Encompassing the westernmost 100 miles of Grand Canyon's rolling hills, rugged mesas, and deep gorges, this scenic reservation is rich in wildlife and home to 1,675 Hualapai, who are closely related to the Havasupai. Tribe-operated Hualapai River Runners offer one- and two-day white water rafting trips on the Colorado River. *FYI:* Peach Springs; 602-769-2216.

13) Kaibab-Paiute: Traditional language, celebrations, community organization and values are practiced on the reservation, located on the Colorado Plateau's rolling grasslands and mesas. **Pipe Spring National Monument**, on the reservation, presents regular demonstrations of cheese-making, baking, woodcarving, and other pioneer skills. *FYI:* Fredonia; 602-643-7245.

Healing Art
Hopi and Navajo sand paintings are part of cleansing and healing ceremonies. Their creators are healers as well as artists. Traditionally, the tribes used colored sands from the Painted Desert and surrounding countryside to create up to 1,200 designs for various ceremonies. The paintings were started at sunrise and usually destroyed at sundown. During the 1960s, both men and women began producing and selling commercial sand paintings mounted on particleboard.

Honoring Spider Woman
According to Navajo legend, Spider Woman taught the tribe's women to weave. To honor her, Navajos left a small opening similar to a spider-web hole in each blanket. The practice was discontinued after Navajo blankets became a commercial commodity, because many buyers thought the hole was a defect.

Southwest Regional Office/NPS

A Navajo weaver

14) Navajo: The 17.5 million acres of the nation's largest reservation spills into Utah and New Mexico, and contains Lake Powell, Monument Valley, Rainbow Bridge, and Canyon de Chelly. Although mineral reserves have made the tribe's 260,000 members wealthy, some still tend sheep and maintain other traditions. The Navajo believe good spirits come from the east, and doorways of many homes still face the rising sun. *FYI:* Window Rock; 602-871-4941.

15) Pascua-Yaqui: The Yaquis migrated to Arizona from Mexico during the last 50 years. Although they are descended from the Toltecs, Yaquis accepted Catholicism and today their religion combines Christian and traditional beliefs. The Yaquis' most important annual event is their Easter Ceremonies. *FYI:* Tucson; 602-883-2838.

16) Salt River: According to Pima legend, the tribe originated from a single chieftain. In the early 1800s the Maricopas and Pimas united for protection against the Yumas. Approximately 5,120 members of both tribes live on the 52,729 acres of scenic desert. *FYI:* Scottsdale; 602-941-7277.

17) San Carlos: Established in 1871, the 1.8-million-acre San Carlos Reservation became a relocation center for Apaches, Mojaves, and Yumas. Stocked lakes provide excellent fishing and the Salt River is a favorite whitewater rafting, kayaking, and canoeing stream. Visitors are welcome at select dances, sunrise ceremonies, and the All-Indian Rodeo. *FYI:* San Carlos; 602-475-2361.

18) Tohono O'Odham: America's second largest Indian reservation encompasses 2,800,000 acres of scenic desert valleys, plains and high mountains. It includes the Papago, San Xavier, and Gila Bend reservations, Kitt Peak National Observatory, and Mission San Xavier del Bac. The landscape of cactus, mesquite, ironwood, and paloverde is shared by Pimas and Papagos, who consider themselves one family. *FYI:* Sells; 602-383-2221.

19) Tonto-Apache: Approximately 100 tribal members live on 85 acres of beautiful pine forest, lakes, and streams. In the heart of Tonto National Forest, it offers hiking and unlimited winter sports. *FYI:* Payson; 602-474-5000.

Arizona Office of Tourism

Navajo still tend sheep amidst Monument Valley's red rock spires

20) Yavapai-Prescott: About 120 of 1,400 tribal members live on 1,400 acres which are popular with hikers, bird-watchers, hunters, and fishermen. *FYI:* Prescott; 602-445-8790.

Hubbell Trading Post, circa 1900

Hubbell Trading Post
The nation's oldest continuously operating Navajo trading post was founded in the 1870s by John Lorenzo Hubbell, who lived in both cultures and dedicated his life to helping Navajos. During his life, Hubbell owned 24 trading posts and served on the Territorial Council and the State Senate. Groceries, Navajo jewelry, rugs, and baskets are still sold at the National Historic Site. *FYI:* Ganado; 602-755-3475.

Pow Wows
O'Ohan Tash, one of the nation's major Native American celebrations, features parades, barbecues, Indian ceremonial dances, and an all-Indian rodeo. *FYI:* Casa Grande; 602-836-4723. **Apache JII Day,** an all-Indian celebration and the only festival dedicated to the Apache people, includes Indian food booths, crafts, and paintings. *FYI:* Globe; 800-448-8983. The **Navajo Nation Fair** offers five days of music, an all-Indian rodeo, world renowned Indian artisans, and arts and crafts. *FYI:* Window Rock; 602-871-6478. Over 75 tribes sell their wares at the **Pueblo Grande Indian Market**, where Native American singers and dancers, fry bread, and chili are specialties. *FYI:* Phoenix; 602-495-0901.

Hispanic Cultures

The sights, sounds, and aromas of Hispanic cultures are never very far away in Arizona. Mexican adobe and Spanish architecture grace churches, homes, businesses, and shopping malls. Major Mexican festivals are statewide celebrations. The music of Mexico can be heard year-round at

Mexican folkloricos are held in many Arizona cities

restaurants, lounges, and festivals. Mexican folk-dance troupes are found throughout Arizona. The 1,560,000 visitors that come to Arizona from Mexico each year rank first in numbers and total tourism expenditures.

Spaniards were the first Europeans to enter Arizona. Jose de Basconales, one of Cortes' lieutenants, entered Zuni lands in 1526. By 1692, the Jesuits had established the first European settlement with a mission at Guevani, 8 miles north of Nogales.

Movers and Shakers

Arizona's Hispanics have made significant contributions to civil rights and politics. **Doctor Carlos Montezuma**, born on the Fort McDowell Indian Reservation, fought for Native American rights and other issues. **Cesar Chavez**, who grew up in Yuma, helped improve living conditions and raise wages for migrant farm workers. In 1964, **Raul H. Castro** became the first Mexican-American governor of Arizona. He has also served as a U.S. official in several Central and South American countries.

Labor organizer Cesar Chavez grew up in Yuma

Old Pueblo

Approximately 25 percent of Tucson's population is Mexican American. Known as the Old Pueblo, Tucson is one of the oldest continuously inhabited places in the nation and has been governed by Spain, Mexico, the Confederacy, and the

United States. Several festivals celebrate the city's Spanish/Mexican heritage. Many of its buildings date to the Mexican period. Some are listed on the National Register of Historic Sites.

La Casa Cordova, 175 N. Meyer Ave., believed to be Tucson's oldest building, is now a Mexican Heritage Museum. **Sosa-Carrillo Fremont House**, 151 S. Granada Ave, was built in the 1850s by a Mexican family and became the home of Territorial Governor John C. Fremont. The **State Building**, 416 W. Congress St., displays rambling pink adobe and a colorful mosaic of intricate inlaid tiles. **Armory Park and El Presidio**, 100 block of Church Avenue, contain portions of the original 1775 Spanish fort, the Tucson Museum of Art, and four historic adobe homes.

Tucson's Meet Yourself festival is a celebration of the state's diverse heritage

Eddie Goldbaum Rios, Metropolitan Tucson Convention & Visitors Bureau

Tubac, now a thriving art colony, attracts visitors with its shops, studios, and galleries. Tubac Presidio State Park includes the Presidio Museum and other structures where the Spanish established a garrison after its settlers were massacred by Indians in 1751.

In Phoenix, **Museo Chicano** is a Chicano museum and Latino center for the arts. Changing exhibits highlight Latino culture, and the center offers a Latino theater and ballet folklorico. *FYI:* 641 E. Van Buren, Suite 208; 602-257-5536.

Fiestas

Fiesta De San Agustin honors Tucson's patron saint and protector of the presidio and Mexican town, St. Augustine, with a Mexican fiesta, live music, and a street dance. *FYI:* Tucson; 602-628-5774. **The International Mariachi Conference** is North America's largest festival of mariachi performances and a musical celebration of Arizona's Mexican heritage. *FYI:* 602-770-7400. **Mexican Independence Day**, September 16, is celebrated in towns and cities throughout the state with music, arts, folk-dances and food. *FYI:* Tucson; 602-623-8344. **El Cinco de Mayo**, May 5-6, celebrates Mexico's defeat of the French at Puebla, with music, artists, folk-dances, and food. *FYI:* Tucson; 602-623-8344.

Border Towns

Not surprisingly, the greatest concentration of Hispanics is in and near Arizona's border towns. While Spanish is the primary language, most Mexican border town residents also speak English. Although they vary greatly in size and facilities, the towns have an international atmosphere. Visitors by the thousands cross into Mexico daily to buy leatherwork, jewelry, and curios. Mexicans come to Arizona to shop for basic necessities.

International Street in Nogales, circa 1898

National Archives and Records Administration

Nogales, Arizona, and Nogales, Mexico: Sharing a common name, the two cities sprawl over scenic hills and wooded valleys surrounding a pass that has been a major travel route for at least 2,000 years. The cities began as an 1880s Mexican roadhouse and an American trading post. The Pima Alta Historical Society Museum, on the Arizona side, is housed in the former city hall-fire-and-police department. It exhibits hand-powered water pumps and other artifacts. *FYI:* Grand and Crawford; 602-287-4621.

Nogales, Sonora, offers the best shopping and the most visitor traffic. Authentic Mexican food, serenading mariachi bands, and bullfights provide an exhilarating change of pace and an international atmosphere. Local merchants expect to haggle over prices of liquor, leather, jewelry, and clothes.

Douglas, Arizona, and Agua Prieta, Mexico: Unlike Nogales, Agua Prieta's prices on virtually everything are fixed, and the array of merchandise is much smaller. Known as the cleanest of the border towns, it offers charming curio shops, restaurants, and attractive plazas.

The adjacent towns boomed in 1900 when Phelps Dodge Company built a copper smelter at Douglas and named it for the company president. In 1916, Douglas was shelled by Mexicans and became a staging area for General "Black Jack" Pershing's unsuccessful expedition into Mexico to capture Pancho Villa. Douglas was the departure point for the first airplanes used in battle and for the U.S, horse cavalry's final campaign as an independent unit against an enemy. In 1928, America's first international airport opened here.

Lukeville, Arizona, and Sonoita, Mexico: Lukeville, Arizona, has an immigration and customs office, a gas station, store, and motel/trailer park. Several restaurants, motels, and curio shops surround an attractive plaza in Sonoita.

Yuma, Arizona, and San Luis, Mexico: San Luis, the former farming community and port of entry, is 23 miles south of Yuma. With 150,000 people, San Luis is the largest city in Sonora, Mexico. Local artisans are famous for their fine leather products. Clothing, blankets, carved onyx chess sets, and other Mexican products are also readily available.

Crossing the Border

At Nogales and Douglas you can park on the U.S. side and stroll across the border to Mexico's shops. Sonoita lies two miles south of the boundary. United States citizens do not need passports for visits of less than 72 hours and within 75 miles of the border. You can bring up to $400 of Mexican merchandise per person per month back through U.S. Customs. To be safe, check with Customs before you buy: duty-free product lists change frequently, sometimes from month to month. Items that are not duty-free or pose problems include pharmaceuticals, fruits and vegetables, and live birds.

In 1916, General "Black Jack" Pershing's punitive expedition against Pancho Villa was launched from Douglas

Library of Congress

GOING TO TOWN

Phoenix
Pop. 983,403   **Elev.** 1,132 feet
Noted for: State capitol; "Resort Capital of the World"; retirement communities; Heard Museum; golf courses; Phoenix Art Museum; South Mountain Municipal Park; Desert Botanical Garden; Phoenix Suns; Phoenix Cardinals; NASCAR Winston Cup 500.
Nearby: Casa Grande National Monument; Fort McDowell, Gila River, and Salt River Indian Reservations; Lost Dutchman State Park; Squaw Peak, Echo Canyon Recreation Areas; Papago Park/ Hole in the Rock.
Visitor's Information: 602-254-6500.

In the 1860s, Jack Swilling built an irrigation system using remnants of Hohokam canals which had been built from A.D. 350–1450. English scholar Darrell Duppa saw the new civilization rising from the old and suggested naming the town after the mythical bird which was consumed by fire and arose from its own ashes.

Beginning as a Fort McDowell hay camp, Phoenix grew slowly until the railroad arrived in 1887. It became the territorial capital in 1889.

During the 1980s Phoenix attracted over 100,000 newcomers per year, making it the fastest growing area in the country. As retirees and high-tech and other manufacturers discovered its sunny climate, cultural centers, and streets lined with orange, grapefruit and palm trees, it quickly became America's ninth-largest city.

Phoenix voters passed the largest municipal bond measure in United States history in 1988 by approving $1.1 billion for construction of major cultural, recreational, and public-service projects. Today, outstanding museums interpret everything from prehistoric cultures and fine art to fire-fighting and science. The Phoenix Little Theater, founded in 1920, is one of the nation's longest continuously operating community theaters.

Arizona Office of Tourism

Phoenix city center

Tucson
Pop. 405,390   **Elev.** 2,389 feet
Noted for: Arizona-Sonora Desert Museum; University of Arizona; Mission San Xavier del Bac; Old Tucson Studios; St. Augustine Cathedral; Pima Air and Space Museum; Flandrau Science Center and Planetarium; Tucson Museum of Art; "Astronomy Capital of the World."

Tucson Convention Center

C. Cupito, Metropolitan Tucson Convention & Visitors Bureau

Nearby: Saguaro Cactus National Monument; Biosphere 2; Mt. Lemmon Ski Valley; Titan Missile Museum; Sabino Canyon; Kitt Peak National Observatory; Coronado National Forest; Tumacacori National Monument; Colossal Cave; Catalina State Park.
Visitor's Information: 602-624-1817.

Tucson was founded on August 20, 1775 as a walled Spanish presidio, and took its name from a Pima Indian word meaning "spring at the foot of the black mountain." After Mexico ceded Tucson to the United States in 1846, the Butterfield Overland Stagecoach began serving the town, and Anglos soon followed. The settlement prospered as a rip-roaring frontier town in which gunfights were common, then settled down to become the territorial capital. When the first train arrived in 1880, over 7,000 people lived in Tucson. Although it lost the capital in 1877, it gained the University of Arizona.

Tucson lies in a valley surrounded by the Santa Catalina, Sierrita, Santa Rita, and Rincon mountain ranges. It mixes traditional Mexican building techniques with contemporary architecture, and national with international companies. Arizona State Museum on the university campus exhibits artifacts from 10,000 years of regional life. Eighteen campus buildings are listed on the National Register of Historic Places.

Tucson Events
February: Tucson Gem and Mineral Show; La Fiesta de los Vaqueros.
April: Tucson International Mariachi Conference.

Valley of the Sun

Surrounded by cactus-laden mountains rising from 3,000 to 8,000 feet, the Phoenix metropolitan area and its 2.2 million inhabitants spread along the banks of the Salt River, through flat desert, and over rolling hills. Collectively called the Valley of the Sun, the 9,127-square-mile area includes 22 incorporated cities. Behind only Phoenix and Tucson, the Valley's five largest cities are:

Mesa: Arizona's third-largest city (pop. 288,091), Mesa perches on a plateau 12 miles southeast of Phoenix. Founded by Mormons in 1878, its wide streets originally accommodated wagons pulled by long strings of oxen and mules. The Mormon temple has been called one of the most beautiful ecclesiastical structures in the nation, and its gardens are among the most magnificent in the state. **Noted for:** Mesa Southwest Museum, Park of the Canals, Champlin Fighter Museum, Chicago Cubs winter baseball. *FYI:* Chamber of Commerce; 602-969-1307.

Glendale: Between 1970 and 1988, Glendale grew 388 percent to 148,134 people. Established in 1892 by a land company for the Church of the Brethren of Illinois, today it claims the state's greatest concentration of antique shops. **Noted for:** Catlin Court Historical District, National Register of Historic Places Sahuaro Ranch, Thunderbird Balloon Classic and Air Show. *FYI:* Chamber of Commerce; 602-937-4754.

Tempe: Established in 1871 when Charles Turnbull Hayden started a ferry service, flour mill, and mercantile store, Tempe today is a city of 141,865. The Hayden flour mill is the oldest continuously operating business in Arizona. A walking tour includes buildings and architectural styles dating to the turn of the century. **Noted for:** Arizona State University (the largest enrollment of any Southwestern university); sports (including Phoenix Cardinals football, Phoenix Suns basketball, the Fiesta Bowl, and Cactus League baseball); Grady Grammage Memorial Auditorium; Peterson House Museum, Old Town Tempe Spring and Fall

Arizona Office of Tourism

Glendale's Thunderbird Balloon Classic is one of many events that draw visitors to the Valley of the Sun

Several major rodeos are held in Valley communities

Phoenix Convention Bureau

Festivals. *FYI:* Visitor's Bureau; 602-894-8158. **Scottsdale:** Named for Army Chaplain Winfield Scott, who homesteaded the area in 1888, Scottsdale calls itself "The West's Most Western Town." Some small-town trappings disappeared as Scottsdale grew from 2,000 people and one square mile in 1951 to 183 square miles and 130,069 people today and became a refuge for artists and visitors escaping harsh northern winters. **Noted for:** American Heritage Wax Museum; galleries and boutiques; Scottsdale Mall, one of the nation's largest; Parada del Sol, one of the largest professional winter rodeos; Consanti Foundation; Frank Lloyd Wright Foundation; Buffalo Museum of America; Rawhide 1880s Western Town; Camelback Mountain, Phoenix Open Golf Tournament. *FYI:* Chamber of Commerce; 602-945-8481. **Chandler**: With a population of 90,533, Chandler is Arizona's seventh-largest city. Dr. Alexander John Chandler, Arizona Territory's first veterinary surgeon, steered its incorporation in 1920. Although it was one of the nation's first planned communities, Chandler soon became a thriving agricultural area. Today it's also the Milwaukee Brewers' spring training home. The Chandler Center for the Arts offers ballet, opera, comedy, and concerts. **Noted for:** Annual Tumbleweed Christmas Tree Lighting Ceremony featuring the world's largest Tumbleweed Christmas Tree; Ostrich Festival. *FYI:* Chamber of Commerce; 602-892-0056.

Sedona

Pop. 14,500   **Elev.** 4,500 feet

Noted for: Spectacular red-rock country; art galleries; shopping; vortexes; Oak Creek Canyon; Chapel of the Holy Cross; restaurants.

Nearby: Slide Rock State Park; Red Rock State Park; Jerome; Montezuma Castle National Monument; Fort Verde Historic Park; Tuzigoot National Monument; Verde River Canyon.

Visitor's Information: 602-282-7722; outside Arizona, 800-ATT-SEDONA.

Sedona's famed red rocks

Arizona Office of Tourism

In the shadow of the Mogollon Rim, surrounded by spectacular red-rock formations, Sedona has become the darling of New Agers, artists, celebrities, filmmakers, and upscale retired people.

The town reached lofty heights from inauspicious beginnings. Although the first Anglos arrived in 1876, the remote area had attracted only 20 families by the turn of the century. When farmer T. C. Schnebly opened a post office in 1902, he named it for his wife Sedona.

In 1950, Sedona (the town, not the wife) attracted surrealist painter Max Ernst, and other artists followed. The Cowboy Artists of America was organized here, and today more than 40 galleries exhibit a wide range of arts and crafts, Indian art, sculptures, and paintings.

The canyons and blazing red rocks surrounding the town have served as backdrops for hundreds of western movies and television shows. You may have seen them framing John Wayne in *Angel and the Badman*, Burt Lancaster in *The Scalp Hunters*, and Robert DeNiro in *Midnight Run*. Idyllic Oak Creek Canyon is home to over a dozen threatened bird species, and 26 other species nest in the area.

Sedona Festivals and Events

June: Sedona Chamber Music Festival; Native American
    Youth Art Fair.
September: Jazz on the Rocks.
October: Fiesta del Tlaquepaque.

Flagstaff
Pop. 45,857 **Elev.** 6,905 feet
Noted for: Northern Arizona University Art Museum; Coconino Center For the Arts; Riordan Mansion State Park; Pioneer Historical Museum; Walnut Canyon National Monument; San Francisco Peaks; Lowell Observatory; National Forest hiking, camping.
Nearby: Oak Creek Canyon, Sunset Crater and Wupatki National Monuments; Snowbowl Ski Area; Meteor Crater; Coconino and Kaibab National Forests.
Visitor's Information: 602-774-4505; outside Arizona, 800-842-7293.

Dottie Blair

Lowell Observatory's observations led to the discovery of Pluto

Northern Arizona's largest city sits in the foothills of the San Francisco Peaks, surrounded by the world's largest stand of ponderosa pines. Flagstaff owes its existence to loggers but its first settler was sheepherder Thomas McMillian, who arrived in 1876 and built a log home which still stands. In 1882, when a sawmill began cutting railroad ties, Flagstaff became the main Arizona stop on the transcontinental line. The city survived three devastating fires to become the Coconino County Seat and the home of Lowell Observatory.

Today timber is harvested on a sustained-yield basis and supports a vibrant wood-products industry. Flagstaff hosts many concerts, plays, and art festivals. An All-Indian Pow Wow, begun in 1929, attracts 10,000 people annually and is one of the nation's most popular Indian events.

Flagstaff received its name when branches were stripped from a tall pine tree so the American flag could be flown on July 4, 1876. Afterwards, the naked tree served as a marker for California-bound wagon trains.

Flagstaff Festivals
June: Route 66 Festival; Festival of Native American Arts; All Indian Pow Wow.
August: Festival in the Pines.

Wickenburg
Pop. 4,515   **Elev.** 2,100 feet
Noted for: Historic buildings; Jail Tree; Desert Caballeros Western Museum; art galleries; hiking; scenic canyons; "Guest Ranch Capital of the World."
Nearby: Hassayampa River Preserve; Box Canyon; Vulture Peak gold mine; Joshua Forest; Weaverville; Stanton; Octave; and Congress ghost towns.
Visitor's Information: 602-684-5479.

If Henry Wickenburg's burro hadn't been so ornery, the town may never have been born. Back in 1864, Wickenburg became so angry with the recalcitrant animal that he threw stones at it. The rocks contained gold, and his Vulture Mine was heralded as Arizona's greatest strike. Soon miners were picking and panning in the surrounding hills. At the height of activity, 80 mines yielded their treasures and Wickenburg was one of Arizona's largest towns.

Wickenburg has an abundance of historic buildings

Wickenburg Chamber of Commerce

During the first 15 years, 400 men, women, and children died in Indian attacks. Because there was no jail, prisoners were chained to a tree, which still stands near the Hassayampa River. (Incidentally, an old legend spawned the saying that "he who drinks the waters of the Hassayampa will nevermore tell the truth." Despite its shortcomings, Wickenburg missed becoming the territorial capital by only two votes.

Some 345 days of sunshine each year and a plethora of guest ranches keep visitors returning. Twenty buildings dating from 1863 to 1922 line Frontier Street. The Desert Caballeros Western Museum preserves Arizona history and art with permanent collections of Native American and nineteenth-century western paintings and sculptures. *FYI:* 602-684-2272.

Wickenburg Events
February: Gold Rush Days.
December: Cowboy Poetry Gathering.

Prescott
Pop. 27,050   **Elev.** 5,347 feet
Noted for: Territorial capital and governor's log mansion; Sharlot
Hall Museum; Bead Museum; Phippen Museum of Western Art;
historic statues; historic district; "Cowboy Capital of the World."
Nearby: Fort Whipple; Prescott National Forest; Jerome.
Visitor's Information: 602-445-2000; outside Arizona, 800-477-0046.

The Arizona Territory was created and Prescott was founded
because Abraham Lincoln wanted Arizona's gold to help finance
the Civil War. Rich in minerals, and relatively free of Confederate
sympathizers, the area met the requirement that the capital be at
or near Fort Whipple. A two-story territorial-governor's log "mansion," which still stands, was built and the city that grew up
around it was named for historian William Hickman Prescott.

Unlike most Arizona
towns, Prescott was built
of wood, rather than
adobe, and was inhabited
mostly by Euro-American
settlers. Tree-lined streets
and a white granite courthouse reflect its pioneers'
midwestern and New
England backgrounds.

From 1867 to 1889,
the capital bounced from
Prescott to Tucson, then
back to Prescott, before
settling in Phoenix.

Prescott

Meanwhile Prescott boomed, thanks to an economy based in bank-
ing, mining, agriculture, lumber, and ranching. The first rodeo in
which cowboys competed for prize money was held here in 1888.

Most of the business district went up in flames in 1900 when
a drunken miner overturned a candle. Many of today's Victorian
homes and a resurrected Whiskey Row were built after that fire.

Prescott Events
June: Territorial Prescott Days, All-Indian Pow Wow.
July: Frontier Days Rodeo.
August: Cowboy Poets Gathering.

Tombstone

Pop. 1,220   **Elev.** 4,539 feet
Noted for: OK Corral; Boot
Hill Graveyard; Tombstone
Courthouse State Historic
Park; Crystal Palace Saloon;
Bird Cage Theater; world's
largest rose tree.
Nearby: Fort Huachuca;
Ramsey Canyon; Coronado
National Memorial; San
Pedro Riparian National
Conservation Area; Bisbee.
Visitor's Information:
Tourism Association, 602-
457-2211.

Many of Tombstone's buildings date back to its glory days

Arizona Office of Tourism

In 1877, when Ed Scheffelein headed into the Arizona wilderness, he was told he would find nothing except his tombstone. Instead he found silver and named the mining town Tombstone. Its saloons and gambling houses entertained thousands of fortune hunters and some of the west's most notorious gamblers and gunfighters. Wyatt Earp, Doc Holliday, Johnny Ringo, and others helped Tombstone earn its slogan: "The town too tough to die."

In 1886–87, flooding in the mines ended Tombstone's glory days. It lives on as a tourist attraction, health center, and winter resort. Some historic buildings still stand, and Boot Hill Cemetery contains the graves of famous outlaws.

Tombstone Events

March: Territorial Days.
May: Wyatt Earp Days.
October: Helldorado Days.

Gunfight at the OK Corral

The West's most famous gunfight took place in Tombstone on October 26, 1881, when Wyatt Earp, his brothers, and Doc Holliday fought the Clanton and McLowry clans. Although novelists and movies generally cast the Earps as good guys, in reality the participants represented a mixed bag of morality. The motives involved politics, rustling, and jealousy over women. Unlike movie versions, the real altercation lasted only about 30 seconds. The event took place in a vacant lot, near but not in the corral. Some participants may have been unarmed.

Jerome

Pop. 403   **Elev.** 4,981–5,250 feet

Noted for: Historic buildings; mine tunnels; art galleries; Jerome State Historic Park; Gold King Mine Museum; camping; hiking; hang gliding.

Nearby: Tuzigoot National Monument; Montezuma Castle National Monument; Fort Verde; Verde River; Dead Horse Ranch State Park; Prescott National Forest.

Visitor's Information: 602-634-2900.

Arizona State Parks

Jerome State Historic Park interprets the town's past with ore stamping machines and three-dimensional models of the town and mines

Jerome's buildings perch precariously along the steep slopes of Mingus Mountain's Cleopatra Hill. Its fortunes have risen and fallen with copper prices, fires, and tourism.

In 1876, three prospectors staked copper claims but lacked the resources to develop them. Eugene Jerome, a cousin of Winston Churchill's mother, had the money and agreed to underwrite the development, providing the town were named after him. Jerome's venture folded in two years, but was revived when William A. Clark invested his vast financial resources and built a narrow gauge railroad to reduce freight costs.

Mines opened and closed with fluctuating copper prices. Several fires and floods destroyed the town. Underground blasting shook the earth so violently that the jail slid downhill 200 feet. Numerous saloons, gambling dens, and brothels earned Jerome the title of "Wickedest Town in the West."

By 1916 Jerome's two bonanza mines had made it Arizona's fifth-largest city. Copper production peaked in 1929, then nose-dived during the Depression. Jerome never recovered. Mine production stopped in 1953 and the population shrank from 15,000 to 50. Artists and sightseers rediscovered the town in the 1960s. Jerome's combination of deserted and renovated buildings have been declared a National Historic Landmark.

Jerome Events
May: Jerome Home Tour.

Yuma

Pop. 54,923   **Elev.** 141 feet
Noted for: Yuma Crossing Quartermaster Depot; Yuma Territorial Prison State Park; St. Thomas Mission; Fort Yuma; Yuma Art Center.
Nearby: San Luis, Mexico; gem fields; All American Canal; Palm Canyon; Castle Dome Mountains.
Visitor's Information: 602-783-0071.

Yuma's annual events include bicycle races, rodeos, parades, and Mexican folkloricos

Although Hernando de Alarcón explored the Yuma area in 1540 and Father Francisco Garces founded two missions in 1779, southwestern Arizona's largest city did not develop until the 1850s.

With the advent of the shallow-draft steamboat, Yuma became the area's major river port and the California Gold Rush brought a booming business in ferry traffic. In 1854, an engineering party balked at the $25 fare, pitched camp, and laid out the town. It boomed with a gold strike of its own which yielded between $20 million and $42 million.

Yuma's countryside is often used as a background for movies, and its hot, dry climate attracts asthma and sinus sufferers.

Yuma Territorial Prison

Just How Bad Was It?
According to fiction writers, heat and sadistic guards made "doing time" at Yuma Territorial Prison a hell on earth.

Actually, the prison was humanely administered and a model institution for its time. It had one of the territory's first libraries, and an early generating plant furnished power for lights and a cell-block ventilation system.

Yuma Events
February: Yuma Crossing Day.

Lake Havasu City
Pop. 24,363
Elev. 482 feet
Noted for: London Bridge;
Lake Havasu; water sports;
retirement living; fishing;
Lake Havasu State Park;
champion outboard racing.
Nearby: Lake Havasu National
Wildlife Refuge; Oatman
ghost town; Fort Mojave
Indian Reservation; Buckskin
Mountain State Park.

London Bridge at Lake Havasu City

Visitor's Information: 602-453-3444 or 800-242-8278.

Lake Havasu City is one of Arizona's newest communities. The lake was formed in 1938 with the building of Parker Dam, and the city was founded by millionaire industrialist Robert McCulloch in 1963. Designed as a self-supporting city, the planned community has a balanced economy based on 40 percent light industry, 40 percent resort and recreation, and 20 percent commercial services. Although it is a popular retirement community, the population's average age is 35.

When McCulloch heard that London Bridge was sinking into the Thames River, he bought the bridge for $2,460,000. The 952-foot structure was dismantled, its 10,276 pieces were numbered, and it was reassembled stone by stone at Lake Havasu City. A replica British village of shops and boutiques was built nearby.

Lake Havasu, with 45 miles of shoreline, attracts sunbathers, swimmers, boaters, and fishermen angling for striped and large-mouth bass, bluegill, and crappie.

Lake Havasu City Events
May: Western Divisional Bass Tournament.
October: London Bridge Days.

Arizona Town Trivia

☛ Bisbee is one of the few non-ferrous-mining communities to produce over a billion dollars in ore.

☛ Globe was named for an almost-solid-silver boulder which contained outlines resembling continents on a world globe.

☛ Yuma's Marine Corps Air Station contains the nation's longest aircraft runway. It covers an area equal to 37 miles of two-lane highway.

TASTE OF ARIZONA

Arizona Eats

The way some guidebooks tell it, Arizonans lived for decades in a harsh land that demanded a hardy cuisine. A legendary example of the no-frills food was a dish called Son-of-A-Bitch Stew in which all the meat and most of the innards of a calf were boiled for five hours. No true SOBer, so goes the tale, would think of vilifying the vittles with anything as vital as vegetables and spices.

Arizona cuisine embraces Native American, Mexican, and desert ingredients

Desert Botanical Garden

Today, such basic fare is merely the parsley on the potato in a smorgasbord where Mexican cooking is tantamount to a religion, Indian dishes have survived the decades, and innovations sprout like wildflowers after a desert storm. While some argue that Arizona lacks a unique cuisine, the roasted-green-chile taste basic to Southwestern cooking is one of its definitive flavors.

Like Arizona's chiles and salsas, which range from infuriatingly mild to stopping just short of incinerating asbestos, Mexican cooking covers a wide spectrum of ingredients and influences. It draws from tropics, deserts, and over 5,000 miles of seacoast, and has been modified and refined by Aztecs, Mayans, Pimas, Spaniards and Americans. Indian food offers less variety. But you can still sample Navajo Fry Bread and Tacos, Hopi Corn Stew, and Pima Sa'auba.

Chile Trivia

☞ Chiles were brought to the Southwest some 400 years ago from Mexico.

☞ Chiles contain more Vitamin A and C than oranges, grapefruit, and lemons.

☞ Never (ever!) touch your eyes, nose, or lips when preparing chiles.

Vying for menu space with traditional foods are regional and nouvelle Southwestern cuisines. Spicy shrimp and other delectables offer alternatives to beef in tacos, enchiladas, and other dishes. A wedding of Mexican ingredients and French techniques has brought innovations like chiles stuffed with lobster and fried in beer batter. Using Arizona's cash crops, bakers and chefs incorporate dates, figs, pecans, and grapefruit in slaws, breads, and desserts. Turning to the Sonoran Desert, they use wild plants as garnishes, seasonings, and substitutes. Saguaro and prickly-pear cactus fruit, cholla buds, baby tumbleweeds, mesquite beans, and flour grace everything from appetizers, soups, and salads to entrees and desserts. Invasions of immigrants have brought Russian, Cajun, Creole, Greek, French, and oriental restaurants.

No-nonsense barbecue is also on the menu. And you can still find plenty of Western-style restaurants dishing up the basic cowboy foods of beef, beans, and biscuits which served residents so well during those rowdy frontier days.

Museum of New Mexico, neg. #56990

Arizona is chock full of restaurants that dish up basic cowboy fare—beef, beans, barbecue, and biscuits

Mexican Madness

Mexican cooking is steeped in Chili Colorado and Chili Verde, red and green peppers, respectively. You can also expect it to be liberally laced with lots of onions and garlic.

Arizona's traditional Mexican meal usually begins with deep-fried tortilla chips, and a salsa made of either chopped or pureed tomato, jalapeño chile, onion, and cilantro.

Recipes for chiles, tasty tacos, tamales, tortillas, and enchiladas have transcended the decades. Cooks and chefs have moved beyond traditional dishes and ingredients by incorporating lime juice, dates, jicama, and tomatillos into Arizona versions of Mexican dishes. Entrees such as Chinle Lamb, Tortilla Quiche, and Chilaquiles are pretty much Arizona concoctions.

Native Cuisine

Native Americans have lived in the Southwest for over 10,000 years and have farmed the land for at least 2,000 years. Beans, fry bread, corn, melons, and wild spinach are basics of the Indian table. Others include plants that were introduced from Mexico and Europe by the Spanish—chiles, tomatoes, cabbages, apricots, peaches, and watermelons.

Southwest Regional Office/NPS

This woman is using a stone corn grinder

Recipes for Indian fry bread and Navajo tacos have been around for decades and remain virtually unchanged, except for eliminating the stone grit in the corn meal. Hopi women still make traditional thin piki bread from ground corn in native ovens. Two Arizona specialties are Indian tacos made with grated cheese, refried beans, shredded lettuce, chopped tomato, and green onions. *Sa'auba*—tortillas and onions—is an easy-to-make, tasty Pima breakfast dish of flour tortillas, shredded longhorn cheese, and chopped green chiles.

Harvesting the Desert

The Sonoran desert contains over 400 edible plants. For thousands of years, Native Americans have relied on foods which the desert provided. They ate the saguaro's fresh fruit, dried it into cakes, boiled it for syrup, and made a pudding to increase a new mother's milk supply. They also made jams and jellies out of prickly-pear cactus. Cholla buds, baby tumbleweed, verdolagas, and native Arizona tepary beans were also part of the Indian diet. Today Papagos still gather saguaro fruit and Apaches travel to time-honored grounds to harvest acorns.

Mighty Mesquite

Native Americans found multiple uses for mesquite. Tea was made from its leaves and its beans were ground into flour, baked in cakes, and fermented for alcoholic drinks. The beans also made a great hair dye. Other parts of the plant were used to heal open wounds, chapped lips, and sore throats. And of course, mesquite wood used as fuel added a special flavor to meats and fish.

Wild Things

As people are becoming increasingly health conscious, they are once again turning to the plants of the desert. Verdolagas, commonly known as purslane, is a green which grows as a wild weed and is used as a substitute for spinach or collards in soups and salads. Prickly-pear jelly has become a state standard, and along with piñon nuts

Grand Canyon National Park

Picnics in the Arizona wild are as popular today as they were in the days of this 1910 expedition to the South Rim

it often glazes cheesecakes. Nopalitos, the tender pads of prickly-pear cactus, is served in tandem with strips of sliced bacon, onion, garlic, and black pepper. Baby tumbleweeds are also finding their way into salads.

Cholla buds are among the most healthful as well as versatile desert plants. Two tablespoons of cholla buds provides as much calcium as an eight-ounce glass of milk.

Sonoran Desert Food Quiz

1) Jams, jellies, and cheesecake toppings are often made from the fruit of ____ cacti.
   - **a.** organ-pipe
   - **b.** prickly pear
   - **c.** saguaro

2) Cookies and tea can be made from the beans of ____.
   - **a.** baby tumbleweeds
   - **b.** cholla
   - **c.** mesquite

3) The buds of ____ are marinated, served in salads, and eaten like pickles.
   - **a.** cholla
   - **b.** tepary beans
   - **c.** verdolagas

ANSWERS: 1) b 2) c 3) a

Cash Crops

It's conceivable that some days your entire breakfast, lunch, and dinner—and your attire while enjoying them—come from Arizona. Each year approximately 1.2 million acres of its farmland are abloom with vegetables, citrus fruit, and cotton.

Without water, most land would remain dry desert. Irrigation, however, has turned Arizona into the nation's salad bowl. Lettuce alone is worth about $100 million annually, and the state also grows significant crops of cabbage, carrots, and onions. Arizona is the nation's second-largest producer of lettuce, cauliflower, and lemons, and it ranks third in growing oranges, tangerines, grapefruit, hon-

Southwest Regional Office/NPS

Today's chefs use everything from cactus to snakes in drawing ingredients from the desert

---

Rattlesnake Chili
1 to 2 pounds ground rattlesnake, armadillo, chicken, or turkey
1 medium onion, chopped
3 cloves garlic, minced
2 6-ounce cans tomato puree
1 tablespoon ground cumin
½ 12-ounce can beer
2 4-ounce cans diced green chiles
4 tablespoons ground red chiles or chili powder
Salt and pepper to taste
Optional: 2 16-ounce cans pinto beans
In skillet, brown the ground meat with onion and garlic. Put in large pot or electric slow-cooker, adding remaining ingredients. In pot, bring to a boil, then reduce heat and simmer 45 minutes to 1 hour. In slow-cooker, cook 6 hours or overnight on low setting. Serves six.

Reprinted by permission of Arizona Highways, *Patricia Myers, and the* Arizona Republic.

eydews, and broccoli. Wheat, barley, sorghum grain, raisins, figs, pecans, and dates are also important cash crops.

The railroad town of Willcox ships more range cattle than any other place in the world. In addition to beef and dairy products, the state also markets poultry and eggs, and sheep and lambs. Collectively, these crops contribute about $1.2 billion a year to Arizona's economy.

Arizona Grapefruit Slaw

2 large grapefruit
1 medium red onion, thinly sliced,
  rings separated
Peel of 1 orange, thinly slivered
1 clove garlic,
  finely minced
½ teaspoon sea salt
1 teaspoon Dijon
  mustard
Juice of 1 lemon
½ cup olive oil
Juice of 1 orange (about ¼ cup)
Freshly ground pepper
1 bunch watercress leaves

1. Peel the grapefruit. Using a very sharp knife, remove all pith. Slice across grapefruit, cutting into rounds about ¼ inch thick. Cut each segment apart. (There should be about 3 cups of fruit.) Place in a serving dish. Place circles of onions over the top of the grapefruit. Sprinkle with slivered orange peel.

2. Mash garlic and salt with the back of a spoon in a medium bowl. Stir in mustard and lemon juice. Very slowly whisk in oil. Mixture will be quite thick; thin it with orange juice. Pour over salad. Sprinkle with freshly ground pepper. Cover; chill thoroughly.

3. Just before serving, garnish with watercress leaves. Toss salad at the table.

Reprinted from Honest American Fare, *by Bert Greene, (c) 1981. Used with permission of Contemporary Books, Inc., Chicago.*

Indian Tacos and Fry Bread
Fry Bread
2 cups flour
½ cup dry milk powder
1 tablespoon baking powder
½ teaspoon salt
2 tablespoons lard or
shortening
¾ cup water
Shortening for deep frying

1. Combine dry ingredients
and lard in mixing bowl; mix
well with fingers.
2. Stir in water with a fork.
Knead until smooth.
3. Divide into six equal parts. Roll into 8" circles ¼" thick.
4. Fry in hot shortening (365°) until brown on one side; turn
with tongs and brown on other side. Drain and place between
paper towels.
Spread each piece of fry bread with ½-cup refried beans. Add
lettuce, tomato, green onion, cheese, avocado, sour cream
and taco sauce. Makes six servings.

Taco Fillings
3 cups heated refried beans
Shredded lettuce
Chopped tomato
Chopped green onion

Grated cheese
Sliced or mashed
  avocado (optional)
Sour cream and
  taco sauce (optional)

Mesquite Cookies
¾ cup margarine
¾ cup sugar
½ cup mesquite flour
1½ cups flour
1 tablespoon cinnamon
2 eggs
Cream sugar and margarine
together. Add eggs and mix well.
Sift in dry ingredients and mix.
Bake on greased cookie sheets at
375° for 8 to 10 minutes. Makes about 60 cookies.

Hopi Corn Stew

1 cup roast beef or ground beef, chopped
1 tablespoon shortening
Salt and pepper to taste
2 cups fresh corn, cut from cobs
1 cup zucchini squash, cubed
2 cups plus 2 tablespoons of water
2 tablespoons cornmeal

1. Heat shortening in a large heavy skillet. Brown meat and add salt and pepper to taste.
2. Add squash, corn and 2 cups water; simmer about 30 minutes, or until vegetables are almost tender
3. In a cup, stir together cornmeal and 2 tablespoons water to make a paste.
4. Stir thickener into stew; stir about five minutes to prevent sticking. Makes four servings.

Recipes for Hopi Corn Stew and Indian Tacos from Savory Southwest: Prize-Winning Recipes *from the* Arizona Republic, *by Judy Hille Walker, copyright 1990 by Phoenix Newspapers. Published by Northland Publishing, Flagstaff, Arizona. Used with permission.*

Desert Salsa

1 cup cholla buds (rehydrated, cooked, and cooled)
1 cup cooked or canned nopalitos
½ medium onion
1 clove garlic
2 tomatoes
½ cup chuparosa flowers
1 small can diced green chiles
1 tablespoon salt
2 tablespoons minced oregano
Juice of ½ lemon or lime

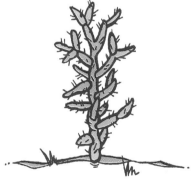

Chop first six ingredients and mix with the rest. Serve with corn chips. To prepare cholla buds and nopalitos: Rinse dried buds, then cover with boiling water and soak for at least 30 minutes. Add more water if needed to cover and simmer until fork-tender. Allow to cool and scrape remaining spines.

Mesquite Cookies and Desert Salsa recipes reprinted with permission from the Desert Botanical Garden publication Sonoran Quarterly, *Volume 47, Number 4, pp. 10 and 12.*

Eating Out in Arizona

1) Mining Camp Restaurant & Trading Post, Apache Junction. All you can eat, family-style dining. *FYI:* 602-982-3181.

2) Harold's Cave Creek Corral Restaurant, Carefree/Cave Creek. Gourmet smokehouse, mesquite-broiled steaks, seafood, and Italian/Continental are all on the menu. *FYI:* 602-488-4173.

3) Garcia's Mexican Restaurants, Chandler. Authentic Mexican dishes served in a Mexican marketplace atmosphere have made this a local favorite for over 30 years. *FYI:* 602-963-0067.

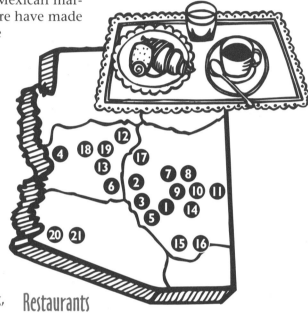

Restaurants

4) The Frigate Restaurant, Lake Havasu City. Barbecue baby back ribs, steak and seafood are specialties. *FYI:* 602-453-9907.

5) Pink Pepper Cuisine of Thailand, Mesa. Award winner, nine years running, for best Thai food. *FYI:* 602-839-9009.

6) LeRhone Restaurant, Peoria. Moderately priced Swiss/Continental cuisine are specialties. *FYI:* 602-933-0151.

7) Aunt Chilada's at Squaw Peak, Phoenix. Traditional Mexican dishes are served in a historic building. *FYI:* 602-944-1286.

8) Tapas Papa Frita Taps/Bar/Restaurante, Phoenix. Spanish cuisine and flamenco entertainment have garnered Best of Phoenix awards for four years running. *FYI:* 602-381-0474.

9) Cafe Terra Cotta, Scottsdale. An innovative menu of contemporary Southwestern cuisine includes deep-fried jalapeño ravioli and large prawns with herbed goat cheese. *FYI:* 602-948-8100.

10) Pepin, Scottsdale. The flamenco entertainment and Spanish cuisine have been awarded five-star ratings from the *Arizona Republic* newspaper. *FYI:* 602-990-7363.

11) Reata Pass Steakhouse, Scottsdale. If you're hankerin' to try deep-fried rattlesnake or mesquite-broiled steaks, halibut or chicken, you'll find them all at this local landmark. *FYI:* 602-585-7277.

12) **Wild Toucan Restaurant and Cantina**, Sedona. Diners have a choice of American or Mexican dishes. *FYI:* 602-284-1604.

13) **Mallaro's Crestview Restaurant, Lounge and Ballroom**, Sun City/Sun City West. Steaks, seafood, and prime rib are house specialties. *FYI:* 602-583-0600.

14) **Rusty Pelican**, Tempe. Eight to ten varieties of fresh seafood are served daily along with beef, pasta, and chicken. *FYI:* 602-345-0972.

15) **Casa Molina**, Tucson. Known for its award-winning Mexican dishes and mariachi performances on weekends. *FYI:* 602-297-5000.

16) **El Mariachi Restaurant**, Tucson. Mariachis provide the entertainment for dining on tequila shrimp, green corn tamales and mesquite-broiled steaks. *FYI:* 602-791-7793.

17) **Cafe Monterey & Cantina**, Verde Valley. Mexican and Southwest cuisines are house staples. *FYI:* 602-567-6611.

18) **Anita's Cocina**, Wickenburg. Specializes in authentic Mexican food, beer, and wine. *FYI:* 602-684-5777.

19) **Frontier Inn**, Wickenburg. Western barbecue ribs, chicken, and prime rib are prepared in Chinese ovens. *FYI:* 602-684-9501.

20) **Beto's Mexican Food**, Yuma. This family-oriented all-you-can-eat restaurant features a Mexican buffet, plus steaks and an American menu. *FYI:* 602-782-6551.

21) **El Pappagallo Mexican Restaurant**, Yuma. House specialties are unique Mexican dishes; seafood, steaks, and American entrees are featured. *FYI:* 602-343-9451.

Food Festivals
Arizona celebrates its culinary delights with several annual festivals. A complete list is available from the Arizona Office of Tourism in Phoenix (*FYI:* 800-247-4000). In June, chefs from leading hotels operate from a garlic gallery at Camp Verde's **Arizona's Own Garlic Festival.** If your first love is chile, you can sample it in April at Bullhead City's **Arizona State Championship Chile Cook-off,** and visit Tucson's Botanical Gardens in October for the **Fiesta de los Chiles,** which also features mariachi, jazz, blues, and bluegrass bands.

From the Vine

Arizonans have been sampling the grape since the 1600s when Father Kino planted vines along the Santa Cruz River. When explorer Bautista de Anza headed west in the 1700s, he planted Arizona rootstock in California.

By the early 1900s there were over ten wineries in the Phoenix, Chandler, and Nogales areas. After Prohibition, Arizona grew only table grapes until the 1980s.

A University of Arizona professor jump-started Arizona's wine industry in 1979 by planting experimental crops of cabernet sauvignon, chenin blanc, pinot noir, and sauvignon blanc near Sonoita. Official recognition came in 1984, when the Sonoita Basin was named a viticultural area by the Bureau of Alcohol, Tobacco, and Firearms.

Today over 300 acres of vineyards produce wine grapes in the Sonoita area. At elevations of 4,000 to 5,000 feet, the climate is almost identical to France's Burgundy region. Daytime temperatures in the low 90s and nights in the low 60s slow the ripening and develop the grapes varietal character. The acidic soil, called *terra rossa*, slows root rot. Wine grapes have also been planted in some of the Salt River and Verde Valley table-grape vineyards.

Vineyards and Brew Pubs

Wineries, Microbreweries, and Brew Pubs

1) R.W. Webb Winery: Arizona's first and largest commercial winery, opened in 1980, produces premium varietal wines and offers 30-45 minute tours and tastings daily. *FYI:* 14 miles southeast of Tucson. On I-10 east, take exit 270. North Frontage Road, 1.4 miles east; 602-629-9911.

2) Sonoita Vineyards and Winery: In 1989, Sonoita Vineyards was selected by *Los Angeles Times* wine critic Robert Balzar to provide wines for President George Bush's Inaugural Food and Wine gala. It has been recognized nationwide for award-winning pinot noir and cabernets, and also produces champagne by a traditional "methode chamenoise." *FYI:* Elgin; 602-455-5893.

3) Gentle Ben's Brewing Company: Voted "Tucson's best beer, bar, and patio," this microbrewery features all-natural beers. *FYI:* 841 N. Tyndall, Tucson; 602-624-4177.

4) Hops! Bistro and Brewery: Beer fresh-brewed on-site is complemented by salads, pasta, gourmet pizza, fish, and grilled meats. *FYI:* 7000 E. Camelback Road, Scottsdale; 602-945-4677.

5) Bandersnatch Brewpub: Enjoy pub food and watch beers being made. *FYI:* 125 E. Fifth Street, Tempe; 602-966-4438. **Arizona Backroad Tours:** The tour operator offers wine tours to the vineyards of your choice. *FYI:* 800-967-2227.

Festivals
Among the events that celebrate the grape are Bisbee's **Wine at the Mine** in late May (*FYI:* 602-455-5893); Elgin's **Blessing of the Vine Festival** in early August (*FYI:* 602-455-5893); and Tucson's **Arizona Harvest Festival** in early October (*FYI:* 602-293-5637). All are informal affairs. Instead of cheese and crackers, you're likely to be eating catfish, black-bean tacos, or rattlesnake sautéed in butter with roasted hazelnuts and garlic.

Scottsdale's **Annual Beers & Waters of the World Tasting Festival** features over 200 imported and domestic beers and waters, plus specialty hors d'oeuvres from nine restaurants (*FYI:* 602-231-0500). In February, at Scottsdale's **Annual Beer Gulch Days Festival**, you can sample over 50 home-brewed and licensed microbrewed beers (*FYI:* 602-279-9717).

ART AND ARCHITECTURE

Artists, Artists Everywhere

Perhaps it's all those yellows, ochres, reds, purples, blues, and mauves in Arizona's landscape, which lend themselves to varying shades from vivid saturations to pale pastels. Maybe it's all those lofty spires, deep gorges, sheer cliffs, and wide-open desert spaces. Whatever the inspiration, art and architecture flourish in Arizona and grow like cacti multiplying in a desert. Art

Many Arizona artists take their inspiration from vivid Southwestern vistas, such as this one at Canyon de Chelly

Arizona Office of Tourism

colonies thrive throughout the state; you'll find them in Sedona, Oak Creek Canyon, Scottsdale, Jerome, Tucson, Lakeside, Bisbee, and Tubac. Many artists and sculptors create in both realistic and abstract styles, and use Indian or Mexican designs and western themes in their work.

Art Museums

Scottsdale has one of the highest concentrations of commercial art galleries in the country. Arizona museums and galleries of national importance exhibit painting, sculpture, photography and other fine arts. Among the noteworthy are:

Phoenix Art Museum, Phoenix: The Southwest's largest art museum hosts over 20 exhibitions per year, showcasing paintings, sculptures, and fashion from the Renaissance to the present. *FYI:* 602-257-1222.

Center for Creative Photography, University of Arizona Campus, Tucson: Permanent archives include 60,000 prints by Ansel Adams, Edward Weston, and 1,500 other photographers. Exhibits change frequently. *FYI:* 602-621-7968.

Tucson Museum of Art, Tucson: Comprehensive collections of Pre-Columbian and Western art are displayed concurrently with traveling exhibits. *FYI:* 602-624-2333.

Museum of Northern Arizona, Flagstaff: This internationally renowned museum houses one of the largest and most extensive collections of fine arts of the Colorado Plateau, and hosts annual Hopi and Navajo exhibitions. *FYI:* 602-774-5211.

Coconino Center for the Arts, Flagstaff: Musical performances, fine arts, and the annual Trappings of the American West and Festival of Native American Arts exhibits are part of the variety offered by this regional museum. *FYI:* 602-779-6921.

Phippen Museum of Western Art, Prescott: Collections, events, and exhibitions center around the history and art of the Southwest. *FYI:* 602-778-1385.

De Grazia Gallery Art & Cultural Foundation, Tucson: The Gallery in the Sun, Little Gallery, and the Mission feature original adobe architecture and exhibits of multimedia works by Ted De Grazia, one of Arizona's most successful artists. *FYI:* 602-299-9191.

University of Arizona Museum of Art, Tucson: Major exhibits include some of the nation's finest university collections of Renaissance and modern works, and 61 plaster and clay models by 20th-century sculptor Jacques Lipchitz. *FYI:* 602-621-7567.

Thomas Moran (1837–1926)
"The business of the great painter should be the representation of great scenes in nature," said Thomas Moran. To that end he devoted his life and became recognized as the 19th century's preeminent landscape painter.

Born in England, Moran made some of the first paintings of Arizona's landscape. Largely self-taught, he was successful as both a fine-art painter and commercial illustrator. When he was 19, one of his first oils was accepted by the Pennsylvania Academy of Fine Arts for an 1856 exhibition.

Thomas Moran's Zoroaster Temple at Sunset depicts the Grand Canyon's grandeur

Phoenix art Museum–Gift of Mr. and Mrs. John W. Kieckhefer

In 1871, Moran accompanied a survey party into Wyoming and his painting *The Grand Canyon of the Yellowstone* helped persuade Congress to establish the National Park. Today it hangs in the Capitol in Washington D.C. along with his painting *The Chasm of the Colorado.*

Native American Art

Native American art in all its forms can be seen and purchased at most reservations and in numerous boutiques throughout the state.

One of the best places to learn about and see an original Hopi sand painting is **The Watchtower** at Desert View. The painting is filled with elaborate symbols and a variety of colors which are interpreted in a brochure. *FYI:* South Rim of the Grand Canyon; 602-638-7888.

Phoenix's **Heard Museum of Anthropology and Primitive Art** contains one of the world's finest collections of Native American art and culture. Its comprehensive exhibits include prehistoric and modern artifacts, as well as basketry, jewelry, pottery, Kachina dolls, and fine art. *FYI:* 602-252-8840.

The **Navajo, Hopi, Fort Apache, and Gila River Indian Reservations** maintain excellent cultural museums and display a variety of Native American art.

Public Art

Although Arizona doesn't make a big deal about its public art, you'll find outstanding examples of sculpture and murals in unexpected places.

In 1907, sculptor Solon Borglum's bronze statue honoring the Rough Riders of the Spanish-American War was erected in the **Prescott City Square**. It is considered one of the best equestrian statues in the world. In the 1980s, the town commissioned several more sculptures commemorating Prescott's rich heritage.

Prescott Chamber of Commerce © Lea Kuhn

Early Settlers *is one of several Prescott statues*

Sky Harbor International Airport in **Phoenix** contains the city's largest collection of public art. Changing exhibits emphasize Arizona artists, cultural facilities, and performance groups.

Public art can be found throughout **Tucson**. Works range from curving arcades at the university campus and the Arlene Dunlap Smith Garden, to the Father Kino statue downtown, and a Holocaust Memorial at the Jewish Community Center.

You can also spend an afternoon or an entire day enjoying the five galleries and five sculpture gardens at the J. Russell and Bonita Nelson Fine Arts Center on the Arizona State University Campus in **Tempe**. At the Tempe Art Center & Sculpture Garden, the beautiful outdoor garden showcases large works by local and national artists. Works of over 60 Arizona artists are represented in its shop.

The Madonna of the Trail

If the statue on Springerville's main street seems familiar, it may be because you've seen its twins in 11 other states.

The idea for the statues, called *The Madonna of the Trail*, originated in 1922 with Daughters of the American Revolution (DAR) member Mrs. John Trigg Moss and future President Harry S. Truman. They successfully petitioned Congress to designate a road commemorating famous pioneer trails.

The DAR also wanted to create a monument capturing the spirit of pioneer women who left the safety of the east for the western wilderness. Twelve identical statues were placed along the Old Trails Road, which stretched from Bethesda, Maryland, to California.

Arizona's Madonna of the Trail *is one of a series of identical statues that honor pioneer women*

The 10-foot-high statues were designed and cast by August Leimback of St. Louis and cost about $1,000 each. Arizona DAR chapters competed for the honor of placing the statue in their area. The Flagstaff chapter, the first to raise enough money to cover the cost of shipping and erecting the monument, chose Springerville as the site.

Performing Arts

Arizona's performing arts offer multiple options. You can spend an evening immersed in the sumptuous sounds of a symphony or an operatic aria, kick up your heels at country concerts and fiddlers' festivals, and swing with modern jazz and Dixieland.

The **Phoenix Symphony Orchestra**, Arizona's major orchestra, and Tucson's **Arizona Opera Company**, have both been nationally recognized for their achievements. Tucson and Flagstaff also support premier symphonies, and symphonic groups perform regularly at Scottsdale, Mesa, and Sun City. Phoenix Ballet Arizona offers programs throughout the year.

The soft sounds of chamber music are performed on a regular basis by world-class groups in Tucson, Phoenix, and Scottsdale. For those who want to add nature's grandest spectacle, the Grand Canyon hosts an annual chamber-music festival each September.

More than 20 theater companies bring serious drama and Broadway shows to the Valley of the Sun. On the local level, Tucson's **Gaslight Theater** offers a steady diet of good old, campy, hiss-the-villain melodramas. *FYI:* 602-886-9428.

Phoenix is also an important stop for touring entertainers, ballet and opera companies, and Broadway shows. The variety of venues range from the charming adobe concert hall of ASU's **Kerr Cultural Center** and the outstanding acoustics of **Grady Gammage Memorial Auditorium**, to the **Sun Dome Center For the Performing Arts**, and 20,000-seat **Blockbuster Desert Sky Pavilion**.

The **Scottsdale Center for the Arts** features a variety of performances in theater and film. Outdoor concerts and festivals are held in the Sculpture Garden. *FYI:* 7383 Scottsdale Mall; 602-994-2301.

Festivals and Events

Modern jazz from down-and-dirty to red-hot and cool is played by nationally recognized musicians in annual festivals at Tucson, Phoenix, and Scottsdale. Sedona's **Jazz on the Rocks**, which also features nationally known musicians, is held outdoors. Thanks in part to the scenic surroundings of vermilion cliffs, the September event has become Arizona's most popular jazz festival. *FYI:* 602-282-1985.

The annual **Lake Havasu City Dixieland Jazz Festival**, held the third weekend in January, kicks off the city's festival season. Eleven bands and over 30 hours of music in five locations, three dance floors, music aboard a riverboat, gospel, pianoramas, and banjoramas are part of the festivities. *FYI:* 800-624-7939.

You won't find any electric amplifiers or heavy-metal at Payson's **State Championship Old Time Fiddlers' Contest.** All "old time" music is played acoustically as contestants compete for the right to represent Arizona in the national championships. *FYI:* 602-474-5242.

At Wickenburg's **Four Corners State Bluegrass Festival and Fiddle Championship**, performers compete in 13 categories for $6,500 in prize money. *FYI:* 602-684-5479.

Apache Junction's **Renaissance Festival** takes you back to the 16th century with a market faire, music, theater, and comedy during selected weekends in February and March. *FYI:* 602-463-2700.

In March, Tempe's **Old Town Spring Festival** features entertainment on four stages, a special children's area, over 450 artists and artisans, and traditional and ethnic foods. A similar fall festival is held in December. *FYI:* 602-967-1993.

Mesa hosts the annual **Arizona Polka Festival** in January. In April the Tohono O'Odham Indian Nation celebrates its social dance music with the **Waila Festival**. *FYI:* 602-628-5774.

Wickenburg Chamber of Commerce

Wickenburg Bluegrass Festival

Literary Arizona

Arizona's history and landscape has fired the imagination of writers from dime novelists to poets. The writers, in turn, have added to the folklore and left a lasting impression of Arizona in the public mind.

Arizona lawman Wyatt Earp has inspired many a novel and biography

In 1905, Congress was considering admitting Arizona and New Mexico to the Union as one state. Poet Sharlot Hall wrote a passionate poem of protest which was read aloud in the House of Representatives. Legislators were impressed by her vision of Arizona as a unique land, and later it was admitted as a separate state.

Colin Fletcher's *The Man Who Walked Through Time* offers a naturalist's meditation on the landscape, inspired by a hike through the Grand Canyon. Edward Abbey wrote eloquently of the Sonoran Desert in *Cactus Country*. Oliver La Farge won the 1930 Pulitzer Prize for fiction for *Laughing Boy*, which he based on years of studying Arizona Indian life. Tony Hillerman continues to illuminate Navajo traditions, mysticism, and modern life in *The Dark Wind* and other novels set on the Navajo reservation.

The state's colorful history has been celebrated in fact and fiction. Deputy Sheriff Billy Breakenridge recounted his exploits in Tombstone in *Helldorado: Bringing the Law to the Mesquite*. Walter Noble Burns, mixing some facts with a lot of imagination, told a lively tale of the town's history in *Tombstone*. Oakley Hall used the Wyatt Earp legend as the inspiration for his novel *Warlock*. Earp himself contributed to the legend by telling his story to Stuart Lake, who immortalized him in *Wyatt Earp: Frontier Marshall*. Elliott Arnold melded fact and fiction in the story of Cochise and his relationship with Indian Agent Tom Jeffords in *Blood Brother*.

Zane Grey (1875–1939)

In 1908, Zane Grey settled into a cabin near Payson and began writing novels with Arizona settings. More than any other writer, his descriptions of its canyons, forests, and mountains left a lasting impression of the state in readers' minds. He immortalized the

Payson region as the "Tonto Rim" and used Arizona as the setting for several novels, including *The Call of the Canyon*, *To the Last Man*, and *Under the Tonto Rim*.

Zane Grey

Library of Congress

Filming Arizona

Director John Ford made Monument Valley's buttes and wide-open spaces known worldwide when he used the area in his classic westerns *Stagecoach*, *The Searchers*, *Rio Grande*, *Cheyenne Autumn*, and *Fort Apache*. Ford, who never let facts interfere with a good story, also embellished the Wyatt Earp legend in *My Darling Clementine*.

Operating on the theory that one sand dune looks pretty much like another, the Yuma area has stood in for deserts throughout the world. Old Tucson Studios, built in 1939 for the film *Arizona*, has been the setting for hundreds of movies and TV series including *Rio Lobo*, *High Chaparral*, and *The Young Riders*. In addition to serving as a movie set, it is also a theme park. *FYI:* 201 S. Kinney Road, Tucson; 602-883-0100.

Old Tucson Studios

Many movie and TV cowboys have ridden off into the Arizona sunset. Even the cameramen wore cowboy hats in the long-lived TV series Death Valley Days, *filmed in Old Tucson.*

Literary and Movie Trivia

☛ O. Henry created the Cisco Kid in his short story "In Old Arizona."
☛ Warner Baxter won an Academy Award for his portrayal of the Kid in the 1929 film version.

Building Arizona

If Arizona's landscape has stimulated artists, it has also motivated the world's foremost architects—thus inspiring some of the 20th century's most innovative building designs and changing architecture worldwide.

Today, Taliesin West houses the Frank Lloyd Wright School of Architecture

Frank Lloyd Wright literally created **Taliesin West** out of Sonoran desert rocks and sand. Set in the McDowell Mountains foothills, it was, he said, "a look over the rim of the world." Built as his winter home, it is today the Frank Lloyd Wright School of Architecture. The complex is notable for its unusual forms, rough rocky surface, and innovative uses of textiles and plastics. Since Wright was constantly experimenting, it also provides insight into his architectural thought over time. Tours take you through a vine-covered pergola, past colorful sculptures, and into his spacious office. *FYI:* Scottsdale; 602-860-2700.

Tempe's **Grady Gammage Memorial Auditorium** was the last major building designed by Wright. The circular hall seats 3,000 people, with the farthest seats only 155 feet from the stage. Balconies are detached from the rear wall so sound travels completely around and through the building. A 145-foot box girder supporting the grand tier may be the largest ever constructed. *FYI:* Arizona State University Campus; 602-965-5062.

Paolo Soleri, a Wright student, developed his own philosophy and coined the term "Arcology" to describe the concept of architecture and ecology working together to produce new urban habitats. **Arcosanti**, a prototype for an "Arcological" town, is an architectural wonder of glass, concrete, and steel surrounded by amber rocks and blue hills. It will house 5,000 people,

Paolo Soleri applied his concept of "Arcology" at Arcosanti

their workplaces, cultural centers, and service facilities in a structure which uses large solar greenhouses for food and climate control. Most of it has been built by volunteers. Tour admissions and the sale of windbells (designed and cast on-site) help finance it. *FYI:* Exit 262 at Cordes Junction; 602-632-7135.

Metropolitan Tucson Convention & Visitors Bureau

Biosphere 2 is an enclosed mini-world modeled after planet Earth

Soleri's work is also seen at **Consanti** in Scottsdale. Constructed by students and apprentices, the buildings are experiments in non-traditional construction methods. Both sites offer windbells and original Soleri sculptures, graphics, and sketches. *FYI:* 602-948-6145.

Biosphere 2 is an occasionally controversial attempt to replicate Earth's conditions in a sealed environment. The mini-world, modeled after planet Earth (Biosphere 1), features seven ecological areas from human habitat to tropical rain forest, savanna, ocean, marsh, desert, and agriculture. The system recycles air, water, and the nutrients that sustain humans and 4,000 species of plants and animals. Eight men and women lived in the 3.5-acre glass enclosure for two years. Visitors can walk beside the enclosure and see Biospherians at work. *FYI:* Oracle; 602-825-6200.

Frank Lloyd Wright (1867–1959)
Wright called his work "organic architecture." He saw architecture as a natural link between man and the environment, and believed that buildings should blend with their surroundings and draw inspiration from their settings.

Frank Lloyd Wright Foundation

Over a 70-year period, his concepts revolutionized 20th-century art and architecture. During his lifetime Wright designed 1,146 works, of which 523 were constructed. They included architecture, furniture, lamps, fabrics, carpets, china, silver, and graphic designs. He also designed the Phoenix First Christian Church. *FYI:* 602-246-9206.

Frank Lloyd Wright

Ancient Influences

Architecture is an ancient art in Arizona. Today's amalgamation of styles and influences reflects everything from pueblos to modern

steel-concrete-and-glass structures. Ancient cliff dwellings inspired the pueblo style. Spanish and Mexican styles were models for churches. Many homes, businesses, and public buildings are modified adobe structures which stay cool in summer and warm in winter.

Ecclesiastical Architecture

San Xavier del Bac Mission: Built by Indians, this church is considered the nation's finest example of mission architecture. Moorish, Byzantine, and late-Mexican Renaissance styles were used in its decoration, and the floor forms a Latin cross. Tours are presented daily except Sunday, when it still serves Tohono O'Odham Indians. *FYI:* Tohono O'Odham Reservation; 602-294-2624.

Tumacacori: Massive adobe walls, a fired-brick bell tower, a barrel-vaulted sacristy, and the great domed sanctuary exemplify early mission architecture. The National Historic Park also contains a modern Spanish patio garden and impressive statues of saints. *FYI:* Tumacacori; 602-398-2341.

St. Augustine Cathedral: The beautiful sandstone front is modeled after the Cathedral of Queretaro in Mexico, and features a bronze statue of St. Augustine. *FYI:* 192 S. Stone Ave, Phoenix.

Chapel of the Holy Cross: This concrete and glass chapel, built on a red-rock pedestal, stands approximately 250 feet high and juts out of a thousand-foot rock wall.

San Xavier del Bac Mission, the White Dove of the Desert

C. Cupito, Metropolitan Tucson Convention & Visitors Bureau

Its designer, Marguerite Brunswig Staude, called it "a monument to faith . . . a spiritual fortress so charged with God that it spurs man's spirit upward." *FYI:* Sedona; 602-282-4069.

Very Victorian

Some of the oldest and best-preserved examples of 19th-century Victorian homes are found in **Prescott**. **Bisbee** offers a blend of early 1900s Victorian buildings and 1930s art-deco images. **Phoenix Heritage Square**, at 7th and Monroe Streets, contains a three-block area with the only remaining  homes from the original townsite, plus Victorian Eastlake, neo-classical revival, and other late 1880s styles. *FYI:* 602-262-5071.

A **Tempe** self-guided walking tour takes visitors through an assortment of stylistic evolutions from 1893 Victorian through 1929 Southwest Spanish Colonial Revival. Tempe's Peterson House Museum is a prime example of a late-Victorian Queen Anne-style home furnished with gold-leaf picture frames and hand-stenciled wallpaper. *FYI:* 809 E. Southern Avenue; 602-350-5151.

Uniquely Arizona

Wickenburg is one of the best places to see turn-of-the-century buildings representing a variety of territorial craftsmen styles and construction materials. *FYI:* Chamber of Commerce; 602-684-5479.

Craftsman bungalows from the 1920s, and 1930s Spanish Eclectic and Minimal Traditional styles fill **Glendale**'s Catlin Court Historic District. *FYI:* Glendale Arizona Historical Society; 602-931-5671.

McFarland Historical State Park in **Florence**, preserves the first Pima County Courthouse, which represents a transition between Sonoran and Anglo-American architecture. *FYI:* 602-868-5216.

The ultimate one-of-a-kind is Riordan Mansion near **Flagstaff**. Two brothers built two homes connected by a "rendezvous wing." The rugged exterior of log-slab siding, volcanic rock arches, and hand-split wooden shingles encloses 40 rooms with over 13,000 square feet of living area, designed in the American Arts and Crafts style. *FYI:* 1300 Riordan Ranch Street; 602-779-4395.

THE SPORTING LIFE

Year-round Playground

Abundant sunshine, varied climates, and diverse topography make the sporting life a year-round proposition in Arizona. You can swim in the desert in December and cross-country ski through high mountains in May. Camping, hunting, and fishing are also all-year activities. An average of 306 days of sun per year provides the perfect environment for golf, tennis, hiking, biking, and spectator sports.

Horseback packing and trail rides are ideal for exploring Arizona's deserts, mountains, and back country

Metropolitan Tucson Convention & Visitors Bureau

Golf and Tennis

Arizona has more golf courses per capita than any state west of the Mississippi. Over 8 million rounds of golf are played and visitors spend $120 million each year on the state's 200-plus courses. Famed golf-course architect Robert Trent Jones put Arizona on the golfing map with his dramatic courses at the Wigwam Golf and Country Club. Jack Nicklaus brought the desert into play with his "target style" links, in which shots must carry over expanses of sand and rocks to "targets" of grassed fairways. Arnold Palmer and Tom Weiskopf have also designed Arizona courses.

Many courses and major resorts also include one or more tennis courts. Dozens of schools and public parks have tennis courts open to the public.

Spectator Sports

Arizona's professional athletes tee it up, kick it off, swish it through a basket, and roar around tracks. Professional men golfers compete in the Phoenix and Tucson Opens, The Tradition, and Scottsdale's Tournament Players event. Professional women golfers tee off at Phoenix's Standard Register Tournament and Tucson's Ping/Welch's

Championship Tournament. In World Team Tennis, the Phoenix Smash features top pros like Martina Navratilova and Jimmy Connors.

The National Football League's Phoenix Cardinals train in Flagstaff and play at Arizona State University's Sun Devil Stadium in Tempe. The stadium also hosts the annual New Year's Day college Fiesta Bowl. Winter spectator sports include the National Basketball Association's Phoenix Suns and the Phoenix Roadrunners of the International Hockey League.

Phoenix International Raceway bills itself as "the world's fastest one-mile oval." NASCAR, AMA Superbike Challenge, and Indy Cars try to live up to the reputation. Phoenix Turf Paradise and Prescott Downs offer thoroughbred horse racing.

Cactus League Baseball

In 1946, Cleveland Indians owner Bill Veeck decided to have his team train near his Tucson winter home, and talked the New York Giants into joining him. While the Detroit Tigers trained in Arizona as early as 1929, Veeck's decision made it an annual destination for several major-league clubs.

From mid-February to early April, Cactus League teams and cities usually include: Seattle Mariners and San Diego Padres at Peoria; San Francisco Giants, Scottsdale; Oakland Athletics, Phoenix; California Angels, Tempe; Chicago Cubs, Mesa; Milwaukee Brewers, Chandler; and Colorado Rockies, Tucson.

Peoria's complex features a 10,000-seat stadium and enough practice fields to keep two major-league and eight minor-league teams busy simultaneously. *FYI:* Call 602-678-2222 for tickets.

Rodeos

Professional rodeo started in Prescott in 1888. The state's top rodeos include: Scottsdale's **Parada del Sol** in January and **Rodeo Showdown** in October; Tucson's **La Fiesta de los Vaqueros**, February; Payson's **Senior Pro Rodeo** in May, **Junior Rodeo** in June, and **World's Oldest Continuous Rodeo** in August; Prescott's **Frontier Days & World's Oldest Rodeo**, July.

Prescott Frontier Days Rodeo

Water Sports

Glen Canyon National Recreation Area: Lake Powell is one of the world's most scenic reservoirs and one of Arizona's most popular spots for swimming, water skiing, jet skiing, scuba diving, parasailing, and cruising. The 1,960 miles of shoreline stretches 186 miles through the recreation area's red rocks. With a houseboat, canoe, or kayak you can sightsee the nooks and crannies and explore some of the lake's 96 canyons. Fishermen often limit out on largemouth and striped bass, black crappie, catfish, and trout. Nearby **Rainbow Bridge National Monument** is an easily accessible side trip. The 5.1 million cubic yards of concrete in **Glen Canyon Dam**, which holds back the lake, was poured 24 hours a day for over three years. Tours of the interior are available. **Glen Canyon Bridge** offers a striking view of the dam and lake. *FYI:* Page; 602-645-2471.

Lake Mead National Recreation Area: The recreation area extends 67 miles south from Hoover Dam and includes Lake Mead and Lake Mojave. **Hoover Dam**, located in Black Canyon between Arizona and Nevada, stands 726 feet above bedrock. Built in 1935, it is still the Western Hemisphere's highest concrete Dam. **Lake Mead**, with 28.5 million acre-feet of water, is the largest constructed reservoir in the United States. While both lakes attract virtually every kind of aquatic enthusiast, their immensity means they are seldom crowded. Fishermen enjoy them for the hungry bass, catfish, rainbow, and cutthroat trout. **Lake Mojave** yielded the largest striped bass caught in an inland waterway: 59 pounds, 12 ounces. Bighorn sheep, cormorants, pelicans and other wildlife congregate along the shorelines. While both lakes are usually placid, sudden high winds can create six-foot waves. Visitor centers offer guided tours of Hoover Dam, and commercial marinas rent craft of all sizes. *FYI:* Lake Mead National Recreation Area; 702-293-8906.

Lake Havasu: The scenic desert reservoir is often teeming with jet and water skiers, sailboarders,

Arizona Office of Tourism

Houseboats and speedboats meet and mingle on Lake Powell

sailboaters, parasailers, houseboaters, and fishermen. **Lake Havasu State Park** offers several campgrounds and access to the 45 miles of shoreline. *FYI:* 602-855-7851. Nearby **Buckskin Mountain State Park** caters to Lake Havasu tube floaters and boaters. *FYI:* 602-667-3231.

Theodore Roosevelt Lake: The world's highest masonry dam is the center of a system of impounded lakes that includes Apache, Canyon, and Saguaro Lakes on the Salt River, plus Bartlett and Horseshoe Lakes on the Verde River. Water recreation varies from fishing to water skiing and sailing.

River Floats

Tubing is a major Salt River sport from mid-April to mid-September. A pristine, cottonwood-lined, and usually placid segment of the Verde River provides thrills and wilderness viewing for canoers and kayakers.

The only undammed portion of the Colorado River which is floatable is a 15-mile segment from Glen Canyon Dam to Lee's Ferry. *FYI:* 601-331-5292.

Whitewater

Downstream from Lee's Ferry to Diamond, the Colorado roars through the Grand Canyon, challenging rafters and kayakers with 225 miles of swift currents and thunderous rapids. Professional outfitters licensed by the National Park Service provide 3- to 18-day paddle-boat, power boat, or kayak trips through this section.

Grand Canyon National Park

Whitewater rafting down the mighty Colorado

Gone Fishin'

Arizona lakes, reservoirs, rivers, and streams offer over 20 species of game fish. Many waterways are stocked annually with rainbow trout. Some holes can be fished year-round; seasons vary at others. Live bait is prohibited in many areas. Before you cast your line in the water, pick up a current copy of

Floating the Verde River

the state fishing regulations. *Arizona Fishin' Holes,* published by the Arizona Game and Fish Department (*FYI:* 2221 W. Greenway Road, Phoenix, AZ 85023; 602-942-3000), is available for a nominal fee and includes a comprehensive listing of lakes, streams, and the species found in each.

Fishing the Rivers

Colorado: Since the Colorado and its tributaries drain 90 percent of the state, it also sets the tone for river fishing.

Fishermen from around the world flock to Lee's Ferry, 14 miles downstream from Glen Canyon Dam, seeking trophy trout with flies and lures only. The Upper Colorado also yields striped bass, crappie, sunfish, catfish, northern pike and walleye. Winding south through Lakes Mead and Mojave, the main catches are rainbow trout, striped bass, sunfish, and catfish.

Black: Situated on the White Mountain Indian Reservation, this scenic stream is a good fishery for rainbow, native, brown, and brook trout, and smallmouth bass. Check with the Reservation for special regulations.

Verde: On the Upper Verde in North Central Arizona, the species run to rainbow trout, large- and smallmouth bass, sunfish, and channel and flathead catfish. In the East Verde, along the Mogollon Rim, brown, brook, and rainbow trout mix with small-mouth bass. The Central Verde is a wild area which requires advance preparations but yields big catfish, along with large- and smallmouth bass.

Salt: The best catches in this central river are rainbow, largemouth bass, and catfish.

Bill Williams: This southwestern stream is known for largemouth bass, bullhead, channel and flathead catfish, and red-ear, green, and bluegill sunfish.

Gila: Meandering through the southwestern desert, the Gila offers the same species as the Bill Williams plus tilapia and mullet.

Fly-Fishing

The section of the **East Verde** near Payson is limited to fly-fishing. In the White Mountains area, **Ackre, Christmas Tree, and Lee Valley lakes** are regulated for flies and lures only, as are **J.D. Dam Lake** and **Perkins Tank** in north central Arizona and **Kinnikinick** near Flagstaff. **Horseshoe Cienega Lake**, near Pinetop, offers good fly-fishing in shallow waters and gave up the state record brown trout: 16 pounds, 7 ounces. **Reservation Lake** offers beautiful mountain scenery, and good shoreline and better trolling and fly-fishing for trout.

Hunting

In Arizona, it's open season on some kind of game nearly any time of the year. Game birds include wild turkey, numerous waterfowl, quail, and bandtail pigeons. Game animals range from squirrels, deer, elk, and antelope, to javelina (wild pig), bear, desert bighorn sheep, mountain lion, and buffalo.

National Archives and Records Administration

Hunting and trapping have a long history in Arizona. Here, a father and his sons pose with their pelts outside their cabin near Hell's Hip Pocket, 1908.

Contact the Arizona Game and Fish Department (2221 W. Greenway Road, Phoenix, 85023, 602-942-3000) for seasons and licensing requirements.

Fishing and Hunting Quiz

1) Under Arizona law a hunter is allowed one kill per lifetime for ____.

    a. desert bighorn sheep and buffalo
    b. antelope and mountain lion
    c. javelina and bear

2) The biggest fish ever caught in Arizona was a flathead catfish. It weighed ____.

    a. 56 pounds
    b. 51 pounds
    c. 62 pounds

ANSWERS: 1) a 2) c

Public Lands

Whether you wish to enjoy the great outdoors under a winter desert moon or pitch a tent amidst pine-scented mountains in summer, camping and trekking can be a 12-month experience in Arizona. Two national parks, 16 national monuments, six national forests, 26 state parks, 15 tribal parks, and thousands of acres of BLM land have been set aside for public camping, hiking, and other uses. Collectively, county parks and these agencies offer over 250 campsites, most of which accept both tents and RVs. *FYI:* National Park Service, 602-640-5250; Arizona State Parks, 602-542-4174; Bureau of Land Management, 602-650-0528.

National forests, such as this one near Flagstaff, offer a vast array of recreational opportunities

Arizona Office of Tourism

National Forests

Apache/Sitgreaves: Hikers can explore to elevations of 11,000 feet the varied country of boggy meadows, deep canyons, and snow-fed lakes that run along the Arizona-New Mexico border and north of the Mogollon Rim. *FYI:* 602-333-4301.

Coconino: Massive ponderosa pine forests, scenic Oak Creek Canyon, and the striking red and white limestone walls of the Sycamore Canyon Wilderness are part of this magnificent forest. *FYI:* 602-527-7400.

Coronado: Fir trees, cacti, high mountains, barren desert, and untamed wilderness meet and mix in 12 sections of this southeastern forest. *FYI:* 602-670-6483.

Kaibab: Two sections divided by Grand Canyon National Park, and a third surrounding Williams, offer camping for exploring the canyon's North and South Rims and scenic Kaibab Lake. *FYI:* 602-635-2681.

Prescott: Mountains over 8,000 feet high create a mild year-round climate, a landscape from desert chaparral to ponderosa pine, and spectacular scenic drives on curvy mountain roads. *FYI:* 602-445-1762.

Tonto: Multiple recreational opportunities, natural and constructed, include six artificial lakes, Roosevelt Dam, the Verde River, the scenic Apache Trail, and the rugged Superstition Mountain Wilderness. *FYI:* 602-225-5200.

Mind Your Wilderness Manners

Don't swipe the saguaros. Arizona's cacti and other native plants are protected by state law (and saguaro-nappers *will* be prosecuted). Many cacti die when transplanted. Camp away from water holes and out of areas exposed to flash floods or used by livestock and wildlife. Leave Indian artifacts, petroglyphs, and ruins the way you found them. Don't remove anything living or dead, including fossils, petrified wood, gemstones, and rocks from parks, forests, or campgrounds. Check specific regulations before entering an area.

Ribbon Falls, Kaibab National Forest

Arizona Office of Tourism

Panning Your Fortune

1. Fill a shallow pan about three-quarters full of sand. Add water.
2. Shake pan in quick clockwise and counter-clockwise motions to loosen sand.
3. Start moving sand with rotating motions. Continue, gradually washing away sand and gravel, until only black sand is left. Dip pan into clean water and continue rotating until gold flakes are visible.

Digging Arizona

Arizona is a treasure trove for rockhounds and recreational miners. It has an abundance of petrified wood, jasper, quartz, and tourmaline. Gemstones run from turquoise, peridot, and amethysts, to opals, fire agates, and the coveted "Apache tears" obsidian. Old placer areas still yield gold flakes the size of wheat grains. The area between Wickenburg and Prescott is particularly rich in gold, silver, and collectible minerals. The *Arizona Rock Hound Guide*, published by the State Tourism Division, includes a map of 20 recreational gold-mining areas and gemstone sites. *FYI:* 602-542-8687.

For the Birds

Sixty percent of all bird and animal species found in North America have been sighted in Arizona. Of the 400 varieties of birds, 150 are permanent residents. They range from the comical roadrunner and shaggy vulture to exotics like parrots, pelicans, and stately golden and bald eagles.

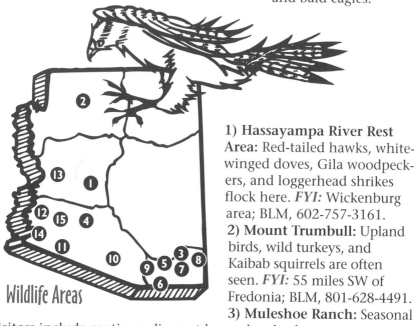

Wildlife Areas

1) **Hassayampa River Rest Area:** Red-tailed hawks, white-winged doves, Gila woodpeckers, and loggerhead shrikes flock here. *FYI:* Wickenburg area; BLM, 602-757-3161.

2) **Mount Trumbull:** Upland birds, wild turkeys, and Kaibab squirrels are often seen. *FYI:* 55 miles SW of Fredonia; BLM, 801-628-4491.

3) **Muleshoe Ranch:** Seasonal visitors include coatimundi, great horned owls, desert tortoise, javelina, and black bear. *FYI:* Near Willcox; BLM, 602-457-2265.

4) **Painted Rock Campground:** American white pelicans, great egrets, snowy egrets, and osprey are often seen at this wheelchair-accessible site. *FYI:* 30 miles northwest of Gila Bend; BLM, 602-780-8090.

5) **San Pedro Riparian National Conservation Area:** Two-thirds of North America's inland bird species have been seen here, one of the nation's best birding spots. *FYI:* 6 miles east of Sierra Vista; BLM, 602-457-2265.

6) **Ramsey Canyon Preserve:** Sixteen species of hummingbirds congregate at this Nature Conservancy site. *FYI:* Call 602-378-2785 for weekend and holiday parking reservations.

7) **Sulphur Springs Valley:** Although over 12,000 sandhill cranes winter here, the site is equally well known for a variety of raptors, including hawks and prairie and peregrine falcons. *FYI:* Willcox area; Chamber of Commerce, 602-384-2272.

8) Chiricahua National Monument: Everything from Virginia's warbler to Mexican chickadees, thickbilled parrots and the U.S.'s largest population of elegant trogons are seen here. *FYI:* 602-824-3560.

9) Patagonia-Sonoita Creek Sanctuary: One of the Southwest's best birding spots attracts over 200 species. *FYI:* Nature Conservancy, 602-622-3861.

10) Buenos Aires National Wildlife Preserve: The 112,500-acre refuge near the Mexican border is home to deer, antelope, javelina, the endangered masked bobwhite quail, and other critters. *FYI:* 602-791-4873.

11) Cabeza Prieta National Wildlife Refuge: This mountain-and-desert refuge is a good place to see desert bighorn sheep, javelinas, endangered Sonoran pronghorn antelope, and Mexican migrants like coatimundis, tropical kingbirds, and over 30 other species. Permits required. *FYI:* 602-726-2619.

12) Cibola National Wildlife Refuge: Over 30 miles of roads meander through the refuge which straddles the Lower Colorado River and the Arizona-California border. Cranes, coyotes, roadrunners, MacGillivray's warblers, and the endangered Yuma clapper rail travel in and out. *FYI:* 714-922-4433.

13) Havasu National Wildlife Refuge: Spectacular Topock Gorge, the desert and mesas of the Bill Williams Unit, and magnificent spring wildflower displays vie for attention with white pelicans, snowy plovers, Inca doves, and numerous other birds. Arizona sections are near Parker Dam. *FYI:* 714-326-3853.

14) Imperial National Wildlife Refuge: Straddling Arizona, California, and the Colorado River, this refuge is a good place for canoe views of antelope, squirrels, wild burros, great blue herons, Foster's terns, and other animals. Rough roads require high-center vehicles. *FYI:* 602-783-3400.

15) Kofa National Wildlife Refuge: Desert bighorn sheep gambol on jagged spires rising abruptly from the desert floor, and mule deer, bobcats, and gray and kit foxes inhabit deserts and mountains. *FYI:* 602-726-2544.

A young peregrine falcon

Southwest Regional Office/NPS

Winter Sports

When you think of winter-sports havens, Arizona is probably not the first place that comes to mind. It does, however, offer many opportunities for cold-weather recreation.

Alpine Skiing

Sunrise Ski Area: Situated on the Fort Apache Indian Reservation, this tribe-owned and -operated resort spreads over three mountains. Sixty runs, with a vertical drop of 1,800 feet, extend up to the 11,000-foot elevation. Eleven lifts carry you to the top. Snowfall averages 250 inches annually. *FYI:* Sunrise Ski Area, McNary; 602-735-7669.

Arizona's high country offers a variety of winter recreation, including alpine and cross-country skiing

Round Valley Chamber of Commerce

Snowbowl Ski Area: The slopes of Agassiz Peak in the San Francisco Peaks contain 32 trails at elevations from 9,200 to 11,500 feet, with a vertical drop of 2,300 feet. If you're not a skier, you can enjoy the 250 inches of snow by renting snowboards. In summer, the four chairlifts are used for scenic skyrides. *FYI:* Near Flagstaff; 602-779-1951.

Williams Ski Area: From approximately mid-December to the end of March you can ski Bill Williams Mountain's five trails, which drop 450 feet from a peak altitude of 8,050 feet. Cross-country ski trails wind through the pine forest, and areas are also set aside for sledding, tubing, and snowmobiling. *FYI:* Near Williams; 602-635-9330.

Mount Lemmon Ski Valley: The southernmost ski area in the United States is accessible via a scenic road that winds from saguaro-studded desert to the pine-capped peaks of the Santa Catalina Mountains. From the 9,000-foot level, runs drop 870 feet. Nearby areas provide cross-country skiing, tobogganing, and summer scenic driving, camping, and fishing. *FYI:* Tucson; 602-576-1321.

Cross-Country Skiing and Snowmobiling

Any snowed-in National Forest service road, unless otherwise posted, is open to cross-country skiing and snowmobiling. The **Pinetop-Lakeside** area's annual Winterfest celebrates the snow season with ski races and other events. **Show Low**, in the center of the White Mountain Recreation Area, is a hub of cross-country activity. **Springerville** and **Eager**, nestled in a mountain valley at about 7,000 feet elevation, are favorites of both cross-country skiers and snowmobilers. Mountain snowmobiling is best around Hannagan Meadow. There are over 200 miles of logging roads and summer roads in the vicinity, and 30 miles of free-use ski trails are marked and maintained.

Although roads are not plowed and permits are necessary, the **Grand Canyon's North Rim** is open to cross-country-skiers and snowmobilers. Other hot snowmobiling areas with magnificent scenery include **U.S. 80 between Flagstaff and Grand Canyon**, **Mormon Lake** (which offers snowmobile rentals, beginners lessons, and guided tours), and **Jacob Lake** (with rentals and tours). The Pole Knoll and Greer areas in the **Apache-Sitgreaves National Forest** maintain connecting cross-country routes.

Ice Fishing and Skating

Mountain lakes freeze to depths of 2 feet, offering rough but invigorating ice fishing and skating. Providing the access roads are clear, **A-1 Lake** near Pinetop and **Luna Lake** near Alpine are popular spots to break the ice. **Hawley Lake**, a popular summer resort on the White Mountain Apache Reservation, is usually the most easily accessible for ice recreation. Several species of trout inhabit the three lakes.

SPIRIT OF ARIZONA

Delight in Diversity

School of American Research, Museum of New Mexico, neg. #15603

The spirit of the Wild West lives on in Arizona

Land, culture, and history have all influenced the complex, continuously evolving spirit of Arizona. Native Americans, Spanish conquistadores, Mexican missionaries, miners, and cattlemen have all left their mark. Arizona has become a stomping ground for actors, conservative politicians, senior citizens, hedonists, and those seeking rest and relaxation—as well as a New Age mecca where disciples draw strength and inspiration from wide open spaces, thermal hot-spring waters, and the energy of vortexes. Thus Arizona's spirit is a mixture of youth and maturity, of coexisting contradictory cultures and trends, of the Wild West and tamed west, of new ideas and centuries-old superstitions and traditions.

Healthy Soaks

Although Arizona's hot springs are few and far between, they have been used for decades and sometimes centuries.

Roper Lake State Park: Hot springs feed this constructed lake at the foot of 10,720-foot Mount Graham in the Pinaleno Mountains. You can also jump into developed hot tubs; fish for bass, bluegill, and catfish; and soak up the sun on the swimming beach. A steep, spectacular drive serpentines up the mountain to Riggs Flat Lake at the 8,600-foot level. *FYI:* 6 miles south of Safford; 602-428-6760.

Hot Well Dunes Recreation Area: In 1928, oil drillers hit hot water instead of petroleum, turning the area into a popular bathing spot. The artesian well produces over 250 gallons of water per minute at a temperature of 106° Fahrenheit. Bring your dune buggy for a romp over the extensive sand dunes and through the rolling creosote and mesquite. Small cattail-lined ponds offer fishing and wildlife observation. *FYI:* Safford area; BLM, 602-650-0528.

Buckhorn Mineral Wells: Since its hot waters were "discovered" in 1939, this health spa has become one of Mesa's most unusual attractions. The combined motel and hot-mineral-water spa features 12 rooms with tubs and whirlpool pumps, outstanding views of red-rock mountains, and a museum displaying over 400 stuffed animals. *FYI:* Mesa; 602-832-1111.

Ringbolt Rapids Hot Spring: It takes some effort and a 6-mile round-trip hike to reach the spring, which surfaces in two artificial pools with temperatures around 100° Fahrenheit. The water overflows the pools and drops about 25 feet, creating a thermal waterfall and a hot shower for those who stand under it. Bring drinking water and allow five hours for the hike. Don't try it during in summer's heat or when thunderstorms threaten the possibility of flash floods. Watch for rattlesnakes. *FYI:* White Rock Canyon, 4.2 miles southeast of Hoover Dam on US 93.

Kaiser Hot Springs: This hot-spring garden sits at the base of towering sedimentary and volcanic bluffs, surrounded by watercress and maidenhair ferns. Crystal-clear springs drop over tiny waterfalls before joining a tributary of the Big Sandy River. A natural bathing pool with a sandy bottom and a picturesque, rocky, tree-lined canyon are part of the scenic setting. No phones, facilities, or clothing requirements. *FYI:* About 12 miles south of Wikieup on US 93.

Phoenix Mystic Madness Festival
Held each November, this off-beat offering features fortune tellers, tarot-card readers, psychics, magicians, astrologers, and palm readers. *FYI:* 602-224-0068.

What's a Vortex?

A vortex is an energy field. Native Americans regarded them as sacred places. Vortexes are believed to have either an energizing or calming effect and to stimulate mental activity and spiritual awareness. At some vortexes, trees lean toward magnetic north and physical facts are reversed. People appear shorter or taller when facing in different directions and water may run uphill instead of down.

Spiritual Places

Sedona: Just about everyone, it seems, finds something to raise or calm their spirits in Sedona. At least seven vortices have been identified in the area. Some, like Bell Rock and Airport Mesa, transmit "electric" energy which energizes and inspires visitors; others, like Cathedral Rock, are "magnetic" and emit calming influences. Several Sedona sightseeing companies offer vortex tours. Their perspectives vary from scientific to self-discovery and incorporate Indian legends and philosophies. Spiritual bookstores and the Center in Sedona . . . All for the New Age provide information on metaphysical events and services. *FYI:* 602-282-1949.

Bob Clemenz

Sedona's Chapel of the Holy Cross lifts the spirits of the beholder

Other visitors find strength and inspiration in Sedona's Chapel of the Holy Cross and at Indian Gardens religious sand sculptures north of town. Schnebly Hill Road offers the majesty of a scenic drive winding high up the cliffs of the Mogollon Rim. The serenity of the countryside can also be explored on jeep tours.

Sabino Canyon: In the last 12,000 years the canyon has given physical and spiritual nourishment to everything from pre-Columbian mammoths to Hohokam Indians and Fort Lowell soldiers. Still an oasis in the desert, Sabino offers a refreshing spot to relax and enjoy peaceful waterfalls, cool pools, and towering rock walls. From numerous hiking trails and picnic areas, you may see various birds, deer, and other animals. A tram system transports sightseers up the canyon during the day; moonlight rides are available three nights per month. *FYI:* Tucson area; 602-749-2861.

Aravaipa Wilderness Area: This Nature Conservancy site is perfect for getting away from it all, whether it's overnighting at a rustic ranch house or exploring the backcountry on horseback or foot. Desert bighorn sheep hug canyon walls and coatimundi forage in canyon bottoms. Permits are needed well in advance of a planned hike into this tranquil 7.5-mile-long canyon. *FYI:* Winkelman area; Nature Conservancy, 602-828-3443.

Thono Chul Park: Although the park was created to promote the conservation of arid regions, it offers a lovely retreat from the hustle and bustle of the fast lane. Wheelchair-accessible nature trails wind through 37 acres of trees, lawns, and gardens. A circulating stream offers cool respite from the heat of the day. Breakfast, lunch, and high tea are served indoors and on a patio. A historic adobe house contains changing art exhibits, and gift shops offer unusual Southwestern items. *FYI:* 7366 N. Paseo del Norte, west of Oracle; 602-575-8468.

Agua Caliente Park: Tucson's best-kept secret was once a mineral hot-springs retreat—hence the name, which is Spanish for "hot water." Along with beautiful views of the mountains, it offers lots of large trees, shaded picnic areas, and water to lift the spirit. *FYI:* 4002 N. Soldier Trail; 602-749-5355.

Courtesy of Bureau of Land Management

Backpackers trek through Aravaipa Canyon Wilderness

Other Worlds

Two of the world's out-
standing centers for
astronomical research
are Lowell Observatory
at Flagstaff and Kitt Peak
National Observatory,
west of Tucson.

Metropolitan Tucson Convention & Visitors Bureau

Kitt Peak National Observatory

Astronomer Percival
Lowell founded the
observatory that bears
his name in 1894. In
1915, he published cal-
culations predicting that another planet existed beyond Neptune.
Pluto, the ninth planet, was discovered in 1930 by Clyde W.
Tombaugh while examining photographs taken through **Lowell
Observatory**'s telescope. This confirmation of Lowell's prediction is
recognized as one of the great discoveries of modern astronomy.

Lowell astronomers were also the first to voice the theory of an
expanding universe, and to determine the temperatures of Mars,
Jupiter, Saturn, and Venus. Visitors can see the historic 24-inch
Clark refractor telescope through which Lowell made his observations. The observatory operates eight telescopes, and offers facility
tours and evening stargazing sessions. *FYI:* On Mars Hill, Flagstaff;
602-774-2096.

NASA

*Lowell Observatory astronomers were the first to
determine the temperature of Saturn*

The most powerful
solar telescope ever built
clings to the 6,900-foot
summit of **Kitt Peak** on
the Papago Indian Reser-
vation. It was chosen
over 150 other moun-
tain sites for its clean
air, stable temperature,
and low wind velocity.
Kitt Peak, which studies
galaxies, stars, and neb-
ulae, is the world's lar-
gest facility for stellar
and solar research. The
21 telescopes, some of
startling size and con-

figuration, comprise one of the world's most important astronomical centers. They are controlled by computers, and sensors convert light into digital images which are stored on tape. A visitors' center and museum explain how everything works. The mountain has picnic tables with fire grills and offers an outstanding view of the countryside below. *FYI:* 40 miles west of Tucson; 602-325-9200.

Mars Myths
In addition to discovering Pluto, Lowell Observatory is noted for its study of Mars. With his powerful telescope, Percival Lowell saw lines running across the Martian landscape; he concluded they were canals which had been built by intelligent life forms. His reasoning contributed to the myth that Mars was capable of supporting life, and fueled the imagination of early 20th-century science-fiction writers. Space satellite photos proved Lowell wrong, but did reveal natural channels which may have been created by running water.

Mars was named for the mythical Roman god of war. Its two small moons are appropriately named Deimos (terror) and Phobos (fear).

Stargazing
The Southwest is the best place in the United States for stargazing. Because of the arid desert, the atmosphere is clear and cloud covers are infrequent.

During the first half-hour after sunset and before sunrise you can see the moon, Venus, Mars, Jupiter, and Saturn. Twilight is one of the best times to observe Earth-constructed satellites whirling through space.

Since star pattern positions shift from east to west as the earth turns and orbits the sun, start your stargazing by watching the western sky. As the earth turns, stars in the west are the first to drop below the horizon.

Ghost Towns

Over 30 ghost towns are scattered throughout Arizona's hills and deserts. Check road conditions before you go; some require high-centered or four-wheel-drive vehicles.

1) At **Cochran**, a few buildings and coke ovens remain from its glory days as a railroad depot.

2) **Dos Cabezas**, once a supply center for surrounding mines and ranches, has an 1885 Wells Fargo stage station and crumbling adobes.

3) **Mowry's** extensive ruins date from the 1850s when the town grew around a silver, lead, and zinc mine.

4) **Paradise** contains ruins of commercial businesses and an old jail dating to the early 1900s.

5) **Pearce** has an operating store, many vacant adobes, and mine and mill ruins.

Ghost Towns

Oatman

The town and mine were named for Olive Oatman, whose family was massacred by Indians. Taken captive, she was later rescued. In 1915, a mining company dug a 465-foot shaft and struck $14 million in ore. Soon, over 100 mine shafts penetrated the area and Oatman grew to 8,000 people.

Wild burros, reportedly descended from miners' pack animals, wander the streets of board sidewalks and restored wooden storefronts. Oatman is located at Milepost 25 on historic Route 66.

Historic Cemeteries

Some of the best places to find historic cemeteries are in mining or ghost towns. Tombstone's Boot Hill contains the graves of the outlaws who frequented the town. Ghost-town cemeteries are found at Congress, Ehrenberg, Gleeson, Harshaw, McCabe, and Signal. They range from well-maintained to Weaver's Boot Hill "where slayer and slain sleep in nameless graves and peaceful anonymity."

Ghostly Buildings

There are at least 12 candidates for the ghosts which are said to haunt the adobe ruins of the **Bronco Mine Cabin**. Several mine-owners were killed by Mexicans and Apaches. Many outlaws used the cabin as a hideout, and died in shootouts with each other or local lawmen. *FYI:* Near Sierra Vista; BLM, 602-428-4040.

The **Gold King Mansion**'s concrete shell with arched doorways and windows stands in a dusty canyon as a ghostly reminder of failed copper, gold, silver, and lead mines. Built for the mine's manager, the 11-room mansion's stairway stretches from the riverbed to the second-story balcony. *FYI:* 27 miles south of Kingman on rough dirt road; BLM, 602-757-3161.

Boot Hill grave markers reflect Tombstone's rowdy past

Southwest Regional Office/NPS

The Devil's Highway

El Camino del Diablo—the Devil's Highway—begins at Organ Pipe Cactus National Monument and ends near Yuma. Surviving the road, which was blazed by Father Kino in the late 1600s, depended on finding scarce water holes and avoiding hostile Indians and bandits. During the California Gold Rush, more than 400 people died along this route, in what has been called a record probably without parallel in North America.

It can still be driven with a four-wheel drive, heavy-duty vehicle. If you go, take plenty of extra water and make sure your tires and vehicle are in good condition—there are no services along the way.

> ### The Trail of Graves
> During the 1800s, so many travelers died of thirst and Indian attacks on the road between Wickenburg and Ehrenberg that it became known as the Trail of Graves.

Lost Gold Mines

Arizona loses gold mines like most people lose small change between couch cushions. Somewhere, out among all those canyons, mountains, and desert are the **Escalante**, **Lost Nugget Mine**, **Lost Quartz of the Tonto Apaches**, **Lost Mountain of Silver**, and the **Lost Sopori Mine**—among many others.

The Lost Dutchman

"Where Weaver's Needle casts its long shadow at four in the afternoon, there you will find a vein of rose quartz laced with gold wire— and you will be rich beyond your wildest dreams." With this deathbed statement, Jacob Waltz kicked off the legend of America's most famous lost gold mine.

Like all good legends, there are several versions of this story. According to most, the treasure was originally found by Mexicans. Either fearing Indian attacks or knowing that the area would soon become part of the United States, they returned with a large contingent from their village. After loading mules with as much gold as they could carry, all but two of the caravan were killed by Apaches, who believed the mountain's thunder gods were angered by the treasure's removal. Years later, the survivors returned and were either killed by Waltz or told him of the mine's location.

"Dutchman" Waltz—also spelled Wolz and Walz—was born in Germany and, depending on the version, was either a former engineer, farmer, or miner. A loner and an alcoholic, he never developed the mine but returned periodically to remove gold as he needed it. Many tried to follow him, but were either killed or eluded by him in the maze of canyons.

The Superstition Mountains

The Lost Dutchman Mine is located somewhere in the Superstition Mountains, near Apache Junction. The mountains are aptly named.

Among the most awesome of North America's mountains, they were formed some 20 to 30 million years ago when earthquakes, massive upheavals, and volcanic eruptions pushed earth thousands of feet into the air.

Weaver's Needle, a gigantic lava plug which stands as a rock monolith, is the focal point for all expeditions which have searched for the mine. None have found it. Many were shot at or beheaded, died of thirst, or became lost and never returned from the maze of ridges, box canyons, and high vertical cliffs.

Legend has it that each one of the bleached-white rocks at the base of the foothills represents a Lost Dutchman Mine-seeker who never returned.

Superstition Mountains

Old West Highway Association

Braving the Superstitions

The 124,117-acre **Superstition Mountains Wilderness** is among the nation's most popular designated areas. Some 140 miles of hiking and horseback trails wind through the rugged mountains and lead to such sites as Devil's Chasm and Aztec Peak. *FYI:* Tonto National Forest; 602-225-5200. At **Lost Dutchman State Park**, you can camp, picnic and hike at the base of the Superstitions. *FYI:* 602-982-4485. The legend of the mountains and the mine is interpreted at the **Superstition Mountains/Lost Dutchman Museum**, along with exhibits on Spanish/Mexican artifacts, cowboys, miners, and prospectors. *FYI:* Apache Junction; 602-983-4888.

Special Events

Lost Dutchman Days, in February, celebrates the legend with a rodeo, parade, carnival, entertainment, and mock gold-rush. *FYI:* Apache Junction; 602-982-3141.

Dons of Arizona Lost Dutchman Gold Mine Superstition Mountain Trek, in March, features a "search" for the mine, a legendrama, gold panning, and Indian and Mexican dances. *FYI:* Apache Junction; 602-258-6016.

One and Onlys

Four Corners: The only place in the United States where four states touch is where the northeast tip of Arizona meets the New Mexico, Utah, and Colorado borders. A monument marks the corners, and at a designated spot you can stand in all four states at once.

Park of the Canals: This is the only place where visitors can trace ancient Hohokam canals, see remnants of Phoenix pioneer waterways, and visit a modern Salt River Project canal. *FYI:* 1710 N. Horne, Mesa.

Palm Canyon: The *Washingtonia Arizonica*, the only palm tree native to Arizona, grows only in this small canyon. To reach the canyon, which is part of Kofa National Wildlife Refuge, requires a tough one-mile climb through rugged bighorn-sheep country.

Nation's Largest Ponderosa Pine Forest: The stand spans portions of Arizona's Apache-Sitgreaves, Coconino, and Kaibab National Forests.

World's Tallest Fountain: The 520-foot-high stream, which erupts for 15 minutes on the hour, has been recognized by the *Guinness Book of World Records*. *FYI:* Fountain Hills; 602-937-1654.

Honoring the Rich and Famous

Tom Mix Memorial: A riderless horse marks the spot where cowboy film star Tom Mix was killed on October 12, 1942, when his large Cord automobile overturned in the ditch now known as Tom Mix Wash. The monument's inscription reads: "In memory of Tom Mix, whose spirit left his body on this spot and whose characterization and portrayals of life served to better fix memories of the Old West in the minds of living men." *FYI:* 17 miles south of Florence on US 89.

John Slaughter's Ranch: A former Confederate soldier, Texas Ranger, and sheriff of Tombstone, Slaughter epitomized the frontier lawman who often shot first and asked questions later. In 1884, he bought the 65,000-acre San Bernardino Ranch and built a sizable cattle herd. Now the San Bernardino Ranch National Historic

Many residents of old Arizona Territory, including John Slaughter, were one-time Texas Rangers

Landmark, it contains 140 acres with a cemetery, barn, and house which have been restored to provide a sense of early 1900s ranch life in territorial Arizona. *FYI:* 16 miles east of Douglas on the Geronimo Trail; 602-558-2474.

"Rawhide Jimmy" Douglas Mansion: Douglas acquired his name by using rawhide to reduce wear on cable-car rollers. He made his fortune in Jerome with his Little Daisy copper mine. The adobe mansion was designed as a combination home and hotel for visiting investors and mining officials. It included a wine cellar, billiard room, and an innovative central vacuuming system. Now a State Park and Museum devoted to the history of the family and the Jerome area, it exhibits artifacts and a three-dimensional model of the town and underground mines. *FYI:* 602-634-5381.

Festivals and Special Events
The **Chandler Ostrich Festival** honors the business of growing the big birds with ostrich races, a parade, science and technology exhibits, and a variety of music. *FYI:* 602-963-4571. The **Tempe Duck Race**, with over 60,000 rubber ducks, is the nation's largest race of its kind. *FYI:* Fiesta Bowl; 602-350-0900. **Welcome Back Buzzards Day** celebrates the turkey vultures' return to their roosts in a eucalyptus grove. *FYI:* Boyce Thompson Arboretum, Superior; 602-689-2811.

KIDS' ADVENTURES

Attractions Galore

Whether it's reliving the excitement of the Old West or peeking through a telescope seeking worlds of tomorrow, parents will find abundant attractions for children and something for themselves to enjoy as well.

Arizona Doll and Toy Museum: Antique and modern dolls and toys appear in changing exhibits. *FYI:* Phoenix; 602-253-9337.

Arizona Museum for Youth: Interactive displays and hands-on exhibits have earned national recognition for this innovative child-oriented museum. *FYI:* Mesa; 602-644-2467.

Desert Botanical Garden: Youngsters can grind corn and mesquite beans, make yucca brushes, and watch for jackrabbits, squirrels, and desert tortoises that creep and scurry through the garden's 20,000 plants. *FYI:* Phoenix; 602-941-1225.

Phoenix Convention Bureau

Arizona's many festivals, from heritage celebrations to hot-air balloon spectacles, offer fun for the whole family

Hall of Flame Museum of Fire-Fighting: Kids can scramble over a 1916 engine and try the hands-on fire safety exhibit, as well as see one of the world's largest collections of vintage fire engines. *FYI:* Phoenix; 602-275-3473.

Phoenix Zoo: An interactive learning center and award-winning children's zoo are part of the 123-acre complex, which features over 1,300 animals, 200 endangered species, a baboon kingdom, and rare Sumatran tigers. *FYI:* Phoenix; 602-233-7771.

Southwest Center For Education and Natural Environment: The evolution of natural and cultural systems is explored with changing interactive natural history exhibits, special events, and family activities. *FYI:* Tempe; 602-965-4179.

Tucson Children's Museum: Ten rooms of hands-on and participatory exhibits focus on the human body and the environment. *FYI:* Tucson; 602-884-7511.

Reid Park Zoo: Small-clawed otters, white rhinoceroses, lion-tailed macaques, and giant anteaters are among more than 300 animals housed here. The park's amenities range from horseshoe pits and swimming pools to a formal rose garden and two golf courses. *FYI:* Tucson; 602-881-4753.

Arizona-Sonora Desert Museum: Underground and underwater exhibits add to the excitement of touring a limestone cave, watching river otters cavort, and experiencing the life of burrowing animals, a prairie dog village, and a bat cave. *FYI:* Tucson; 602-883-1380.

International Wildlife Museum: Through interactive exhibits children can touch and study horns and antlers, fur and hair, and teeth and bones, and learn to identify some of 200 wildlife specimens from six continents. *FYI:* Tucson; 602-624-4024.

Trail Dust Town: Along with board sidewalks and gas lamps, this theme park features a vintage 1940s carousel with 1920s horses and two 1890s carved chariots. *FYI:* Tucson; 602-296-4551.

Slide Rock State Park: Situated in scenic Oak Creek Canyon, the park is a great place for picnicking, camping, and swimming. The creek flows over a natural water slide down which children and adults have been sliding for generations. *FYI:* Sedona; 602-282-3034.

Old Tucson: This Old West theme park, one of the nation's most-often filmed western motion picture sets, entertains young and old with a Kid's Korral play area, rides, rodeos, audience participation stunts, and quick-draw competitions. *FYI:* Tucson; 602-883-0100.

Waterworld USA: Children can cavort on water slides and in a wave pool. The park also offers body surfing and raft rentals. *FYI:* Phoenix; 602-266-5200.

Wildlife World Zoo: The 45-acre facility contains Arizona's largest exotic animal collection with giraffes, rhinos, zebras, monkeys, kangaroos, and 300 other species. *FYI:* Phoenix; 602-935-WILD.

Old Tucson Studios

Children's activities at Old Tucson Studios range from dressing up in period costumes to riding carousels and antique cars

Zoos, Museums, and More

Tonto Fish Hatchery: Rainbow, brook, and brown trout grow from fingerlings to catchable sizes in outdoor raceways and exhibits on an interpretive trail that explains their life cycles. *FYI:* Near Young. 602-478-4200.

Big Surf: Along with surf, sun, sand, and three-to-five-foot artificial waves which crash onto the broad beach, there's a shallow pool for children, water slides, and raft rentals. *FYI:* Tempe. 602-947-SURF.

Rawhide 1880s Western Town: At Arizona's largest western theme town, children can ride a stagecoach, train, or burros; pan for gold; practice roping; and pet ponies and other animals in the petting ranch. *FYI:* Scottsdale. 602-563-1880.

Wexler's Play 'n Ride: Children 12 and under can enjoy a rousing roller coaster and other rides, and play over 60 skill games at this indoor amusement playland. *FYI:* Phoenix. 602-404-2200.

Out of Africa: At this wheelchair-accessible park you'll walk through natural habitats created for lions, tigers, and other big cats, and watch them perform in shows and interact with humans. *FYI:* Fountain Hills; 602-837-7677.

Grand Canyon Deer Farm: Children walk among, touch, and feed several species of deer, pygmy goats, llamas, miniature monkeys, peacocks, and other animals. *FYI:* Williams 602-635-4073.

Museum of the West: Kids are encouraged to search for treasure at a silver mine, grind corn outside a wickiup, use a Victorian ear trumpet, and operate a turn-of-the century washing machine and other exhibits. *FYI:* Tombstone; 602-457-9219.

Crackerjax Family Fun & Sports Park: Miniature golf, bumper cars, bumper boats, and go-karts are among the attractions at this 27-acre complex. *FYI:* Scottsdale. 602-998-5956.

Many Western theme parks, such as Old Tucson, feature special attractions for children

Arizona Office of Tourism

Heard Museum of Anthropology and Primitive Art: The Old Ways-New Ways is a family-oriented exhibit geared to children. Kids can also make cornhusk dolls and other items, and hear

Indian legends in a special children's area. *FYI:* Phoenix; 602-252-8848.

Flandrau Science Center and Planetarium: A walk-through asteroid, NASA space photos, and a hands-on area make science stimulating and fun. Telescope operators assist in recognizing planets, galaxies, and star clusters. *FYI:* University of Arizona. 602-621-4310 for current astronomy information.

Navajo Nation Zoological and Botanical Park: Set beneath towering sandstone pinnacles called "haystacks," the zoo offers a close look at four-horned Navajo churro sheep, rattlesnakes, golden eagles, hawks, elk, wolves, bobcats, mountains lions, coyotes, black bear, and other Southwestern wildlife. *FYI:* Near Window Rock Shopping Center. 602-871-6702.

Mesa Southwest Museum: Interactive and hands-on exhibits allow children to pan for gold, listen to the roar of full-scale animated dinosaurs, see the armor of Spanish conquistadores, and peek into a territorial jail cell. *FYI:* Mesa; 602-644-2230.

Buffalo Museum of America: Have your family's picture taken with a life-sized buffalo model; see one of Buffalo Bill's hunting rifles; and examine collections of buffalo memorabilia including banks, clocks, buttons, spoons, and bronze sculptures. *FYI:* Scottsdale. 602-951-1022.

Arizona Museum of Science and Technology: Interactive exhibits on physics, energy, life sciences, and health; a science arcade; and a mineral display offer something for everyone. *FYI:* Phoenix; 602-256-9388.

Festivals and Special Events
Payson Junior Rodeo, in June, is open to cowkids aged 5 to 18. Events are the same as standard rodeos but feature touch roping, goat tying, and pole bending. *FYI:* Payson; 602-474-6398. Holbrook's **Old West Day/Bucket of Blood Races,** also in June, include children's games and a kids' rodeo. *FYI:* Holbrook; 602-524-6558.

INDEX

Other Books from John Muir Publications

Travel Books by Rick Steves
Asia Through the Back Door,
4th ed., 400 pp. $16.95
Europe 101: History and Art
for the Traveler, 4th ed., 372
pp. $15.95
Europe Through the Back
Door, 12th ed., 434 pp.
$17.95
Europe Through the Back
Door Phrase Book: French,
112 pp. $4.95
Europe Through the Back
Door Phrase Book: German,
112 pp. $4.95
Europe Through the Back
Door Phrase Book: Italian,
112 pp. $4.95
Europe Through the Back
Door Phrase Book: Spanish
& Portuguese, 288 pp. $6.95
Mona Winks: Self-Guided
Tours of Europe's Top
Museums, 2nd ed., 456 pp.
$16.95

*See the 2 to 22 Days series to
follow for other Rick Steves
titles.*

A Natural Destination Series
Belize: A Natural
Destination, 2nd ed., 304 pp.
$16.95
Costa Rica: A Natural
Destination, 3rd ed., 400 pp.
$17.95
Guatemala: A Natural
Destination, 336 pp. $16.95

Undiscovered Islands Series
Undiscovered Islands of the
Caribbean, 3rd ed., 264 pp.
$14.95
Undiscovered Islands of the
Mediterranean, 2nd ed., 256
pp. $13.95
Undiscovered Islands of the
U.S. and Canadian West
Coast, 288 pp. $12.95

For Birding Enthusiasts
The Birder's Guide to Bed
and Breakfasts, U.S. and
Canada, 288 pp. $15.95
The Visitor's Guide to the
Birds of the Central National
Parks: U.S. and Canada, 400
pp. $15.95
The Visitor's Guide to the
Birds of the Eastern National
Parks: U.S. and Canada, 400
pp. $15.95
The Visitor's Guide to the
Birds of the Rocky Mountain
National Parks, U.S. and
Canada, 432 pp. $15.95

Unique Travel Series
Each is 112 pages and $10.95
paper.
Unique Arizona
Unique California
Unique Colorado
Unique Florida
Unique New England
Unique New Mexico
Unique Texas

2 to 22 Days Series
Each title offers 22 flexible daily
itineraries useful for planning
vacations of any length.
Included are "must see" attractions as well as hidden "jewels."
2 to 22 Days in the American
Southwest, 1994 ed., 192 pp.
$10.95
2 to 22 Days in Asia, 1994
ed., 176 pp. $10.95
2 to 22 Days in Australia,
1994 ed., 192 pp. $10.95
2 to 22 Days in California,
1994 ed., 192 pp. $10.95
2 to 22 Days in Eastern
Canada, 1994 ed., 192 pp.
$12.95
2 to 22 Days in Europe, 1994
ed., 304 pp. $14.95
2 to 22 Days in Florida, 1994
ed., 192 pp. $10.95
2 to 22 Days in France, 1994
ed., 192 pp. $10.95
2 to 22 Days in Germany,
Austria, and Switzerland,
1994 ed., 240 pp. $12.95
2 to 22 Days in Great Britain,
1994 ed., 208 pp. $10.95
2 to 22 Days Around the
Great Lakes, 1994 ed., 192 pp.
$10.95
2 to 22 Days in Hawaii, 1994
ed., 192 pp. $10.95
2 to 22 Days in Italy, 1994 ed.,
208 pp. $10.95
2 to 22 Days in New England,
1994 ed., 192 pp. $10.95
2 to 22 Days in New Zealand,
1994 ed., 192 pp. $10.95
2 to 22 Days in Norway,
Sweden, and Denmark, 1994
ed., 192 pp. $10.95
2 to 22 Days in the Pacific
Northwest, 1994 ed., 192 pp.
$10.95
2 to 22 Days in the Rockies,
1994 ed., 192 pp. $10.95
2 to 22 Days in Spain and
Portugal, 1994 ed., 208 pp.
$10.95
2 to 22 Days in Texas, 1994
ed., 192 pp. $10.95
2 to 22 Days in Thailand,
1994 ed., 192 pp. $10.95
22 Days (or More) Around the

World, 1994 ed., 264 pp.
$13.95

Other Terrific Travel Titles
The 100 Best Small Art
Towns in America, 224 pp.
$12.95
Elderhostels: The Students'
Choice, 2nd ed., 304 pp.
$15.95
Environmental Vacations:
Volunteer Projects to Save
the Planet, 2nd ed., 248 pp.
$16.95
A Foreign Visitor's Guide to
America, 224 pp. $12.95
Great Cities of Eastern
Europe, 256 pp. $16.95
Indian America: A Traveler's
Companion, 3rd ed., 432 pp.
$18.95
Interior Furnishings
Southwest, 256 pp. $19.95
Opera! The Guide to Western
Europe's Great Houses, 296
pp. $18.95
Paintbrushes and Pistols:
How the Taos Artists Sold
the West, 288 pp. $17.95
The People's Guide to
Mexico, 9th ed., 608 pp.
$18.95
Ranch Vacations: The
Complete Guide to Guest
and Resort, Fly-Fishing, and
Cross-Country Skiing
Ranches, 3rd ed., 512 pp.
$19.95
The Shopper's Guide to Art
and Crafts in the Hawaiian
Islands, 272 pp. $13.95
The Shopper's Guide to
Mexico, 224 pp. $9.95
Understanding Europeans,
272 pp. $14.95
A Viewer's Guide to Art: A
Glossary of Gods, People,
and Creatures, 144 pp. $10.95
Watch It Made in the U.S.A.:
A Visitor's Guide to the
Companies that Make Your
Favorite Products, 272 pp.
$16.95

Parenting Titles
Being a Father: Family, Work,
and Self, 176 pp. $12.95
Preconception: A Woman's
Guide to Preparing for
Pregnancy and Parenthood,
232 pp. $14.95
Schooling at Home: Parents,
Kids, and Learning, 264 pp.,
$14.95
Teens: A Fresh Look, 240 pp.
$14.95

Automotive Titles
The Greaseless Guide to Car Care Confidence, 224 pp. $14.95
How to Keep Your Datsun/Nissan Alive, 544 pp. $21.95
How to Keep Your Subaru Alive, 480 pp. $21.95
How to Keep Your Toyota Pickup Alive, 392 pp. $21.95
How to Keep Your VW Alive, 15th ed., 464 pp. $21.95

TITLES FOR YOUNG READERS AGES 8 AND UP

American Origins Series
Each is 48 pages and $12.95 hardcover.
Tracing Our English Roots (available 1/95)
Tracing Our French Roots (available 1/95)
Tracing Our German Roots
Tracing Our Irish Roots
Tracing Our Italian Roots
Tracing Our Japanese Roots (available 12/94)
Tracing Our Jewish Roots
Tracing Our Polish Roots

Bizarre & Beautiful Series
Each is 48 pages, $9.95 paper, and $14.95 hardcover.
Bizarre & Beautiful Ears
Bizarre & Beautiful Eyes
Bizarre & Beautiful Feelers
Bizarre & Beautiful Noses
Bizarre & Beautiful Tongues

Environmental Titles
Habitats: Where the Wild Things Live, 48 pp. $9.95
The Indian Way: Learning to Communicate with Mother Earth, 114 pp. $9.95
Rads, Ergs, and Cheeseburgers: The Kids' Guide to Energy and the Environment, 108 pp. $13.95
The Kids' Environment Book: What's Awry and Why, 192 pp. $13.95

Extremely Weird Series
Each is 48 pages, $9.95 paper, and $14.95 hardcover.
Extremely Weird Bats
Extremely Weird Birds
Extremely Weird Endangered Species
Extremely Weird Fishes
Extremely Weird Frogs
Extremely Weird Insects
Extremely Weird Mammals
Extremely Weird Micro Monsters
Extremely Weird Primates
Extremely Weird Reptiles
Extremely Weird Sea Creatures
Extremely Weird Snakes
Extremely Weird Spiders

Kidding Around Travel Series
All are 64 pages and $9.95 paper, except for *Kidding Around Spain* and *Kidding Around the National Parks of the Southwest*, which are 108 pages and $12.95 paper.
Kidding Around Atlanta
Kidding Around Boston, 2nd ed.
Kidding Around Chicago, 2nd ed.
Kidding Around the Hawaiian Islands
Kidding Around London
Kidding Around Los Angeles
Kidding Around the National Parks of the Southwest
Kidding Around New York City, 2nd ed.
Kidding Around Paris
Kidding Around Philadelphia
Kidding Around San Diego
Kidding Around San Francisco
Kidding Around Santa Fe
Kidding Around Seattle
Kidding Around Spain
Kidding Around Washington, D.C., 2nd ed.

Kids Explore Series
Written by kids for kids, all are $9.95 paper.
Kids Explore America's African American Heritage, 128 pp.
Kids Explore the Gifts of Children with Special Needs, 128 pp.
Kids Explore America's Hispanic Heritage, 112 pp.
Kids Explore America's Japanese American Heritage, 144 pp.

Masters of Motion Series
Each is 48 pages and $9.95 paper.
How to Drive an Indy Race Car
How to Fly a 747
How to Fly the Space Shuttle

Rainbow Warrior Artists Series
Each is 48 pages and $14.95 hardcover.
Native Artists of Africa
Native Artists of Europe
Native Artists of North America

Rough and Ready Series
Each is 48 pages and $12.95 hardcover.
Rough and Ready Cowboys
Rough and Ready Homesteaders
Rough and Ready Loggers and Lawmen
Rough and Ready Outlaws
Rough and Ready Prospectors
Rough and Ready Railroaders

X-ray Vision Series
Each is 48 pages and $9.95 paper.
Looking Inside the Brain
Looking Inside Cartoon Animation
Looking Inside Caves and Caverns
Looking Inside Sports Aerodynamics
Looking Inside Sunken Treasures
Looking Inside Telescopes and the Night Sky

Ordering Information
Please check your local bookstore, or call **1-800-888-7504** to order direct. All orders are shipped via UPS; see chart below to calculate charges for U.S. destinations. **No post office boxes please; we must have a street address to ensure delivery.** If the book you request is not available, we will hold your check until we can ship it. Foreign orders are shipped surface rate unless otherwise requested; enclose $3 for the first item and $1 for each additional item.

For U.S. Orders

Totaling	Add
Up to $15.00	$4.25
$15.01 to $45.00	$5.25
$45.01 to $75.00	$6.25
$75.01 or more	$7.25

Methods of Payment
Check, money order, American Express, MasterCard, or Visa. We cannot be responsible for cash sent through the mail. For credit card orders, include your card number, expiration date, and your signature, or call **1-800-888-7504**. American Express card orders can only be shipped to billing address of cardholder. Sorry, no C.O.D.'s. Residents of sunny New Mexico, add 6.25% tax to total.

Address all orders and inquiries to:
John Muir Publications
P.O. Box 613
Santa Fe, NM 87504
(505) 982-4078
(800) 888-7504